Facebook

FOR

DUMMIES®

POCKET EDITION

D0558744

by Carolyn Abram

WILEY

John Wiley & Sons, Inc.

Facebook® For Dummies® Pocket Edition

Published by
John Wiley & Sons, Inc.
111 River Street
Hoboken, NJ 07030-5774

www.wiley.com

Copyright © 2012 by John Wiley & Sons, Inc., Hoboken, New Jersey

Published by John Wiley & Sons, Inc., Hoboken, New Jersey

Published simultaneously in Canada

No part of this publication may be reproduced, stored in a retrieval system or transmitted in any form or by any means, electronic, mechanical, photocopying, recording, scanning or otherwise, except as permitted under Sections 107 or 108 of the 1976 United States Copyright Act, without either the prior written permission of the Publisher, or authorization through payment of the appropriate per-copy fee to the Copyright Clearance Center, 222 Rosewood Drive, Danvers, MA 01923, (978) 750-8400, fax (978) 646-8600. Requests to the Publisher for permission should be addressed to the Permissions Department, John Wiley & Sons, Inc., 111 River Street, Hoboken, NJ 07030, (201) 748-6011, fax (201) 748-6008, or online at http://www.wiley.com/go/permissions.

Trademarks: Wiley, the Wiley logo, For Dummies, the Dummies Man logo, A Reference for the Rest of Us!, The Dummies Way, Dummies Daily, The Fun and Easy Way, Dummies.com, Making Everything Easier, and related trade dress are trademarks or registered trademarks of John Wiley & Sons, Inc. and/or its affiliates in the United States and other countries, and may not be used without written permission. Facebook is a registered trademark of Facebook, Inc. All other trademarks are the property of their respective owners. John Wiley & Sons, Inc. is not associated with any product or vendor mentioned in this book.

LIMIT OF LIABILITY/DISCLAIMER OF WARRANTY: THE PUBLISHER AND THE AUTHOR MAKE NO REPRESENTATIONS OR WARRANTIES WITH RESPECT TO THE ACCURACY OR COMPLETENESS OF THE CONTENTS OF THIS WORK AND SPECIFICALLY DISCLAIM ALL WARRANTIES, INCLUDING WITHOUT LIMITATION WARRANTIES OF FITNESS FOR A PARTICULAR PURPOSE. NO WARRANTY MAY BE CREATED OR EXTENDED BY SALES OR PROMOTIONAL MATERIALS. THE ADVICE AND STRATEGIES CONTAINED HEREIN MAY NOT BE SUITABLE FOR EVERY SITUATION. THIS WORK IS SOLD WITH THE UNDERSTANDING THAT THE PUBLISHER IS NOT ENGAGED IN RENDERING LEGAL, ACCOUNTING, OR OTHER PROFESSIONAL SERVICES. IF PROFESSIONAL ASSISTANCE IS REQUIRED, THE SERVICES OF A COMPETENT PROFESSIONAL PERSON SHOULD BE SOUGHT. NEITHER THE PUBLISHER NOR THE AUTHOR SHALL BE LIABLE FOR DAMAGES ARISING HEREFROM. THE FACT THAT AN ORGANIZATION OR WEBSITE IS REFERRED TO IN THIS WORK AS A CITATION AND/OR A POTENTIAL SOURCE OF FURTHER INFORMATION DOES NOT MEAN THAT THE AUTHOR OR THE PUBLISHER ENDORSES THE INFORMATION THE ORGANIZATION OR WEBSITE MAY PROVIDE OR RECOMMENDATIONS IT MAY MAKE. FURTHER, READERS SHOULD BE AWARE THAT INTERNET WEBSITES LISTED IN THIS WORK MAY HAVE CHANGED OR DISAPPEARED BETWEEN WHEN THIS WORK WAS WRITTEN AND WHEN IT IS READ.

For general information on our other products and services, please contact our Customer Care Department within the U.S. at 877-762-2974, outside the U.S. at 317-572-3993, or fax 317-572-4002.

For technical support, please visit www.wiley.com/techsupport.

Wiley also publishes its books in a variety of electronic formats and by print-on-demand. Not all content that is available in standard print versions of this book may appear or be packaged in all book formats. If you have purchased a version of this book that did not include media that is referenced by or accompanies a standard print version, you may request this media by visiting http://booksupport.wiley.com. For more information about Wiley products, visit us at www.wiley.com.

ISBN 978-0-470-94039-6 (pbk); ISBN 978-1-118-03778-2 (ebk); ISBN 978-1-118-03779-9 (ebk)

Manufactured in the United States of America

10 9 8 7 6 5

WILEY

Publisher's Acknowledgments

We're proud of this book; please send us your comments at http://dummies.custhelp.com. For other comments, please contact our Customer Care Department within the U.S. at 877-762-2974, outside the U.S. at 317-572-3993, or fax 317-572-4002.

Some of the people who helped bring this book to market include the following:

Acquisitions and Editorial

Project Editor: Brian H. Walls
(Previous Edition: Nicole Sholly)

Executive Editor: Steve Hayes

Copy Editor: Annie Sullivan

Technical Editor: Steven Worden

Editorial Manager:
Kevin Kirschner

Editorial Assistant:
Amanda Graham

Sr. Editorial Assistant:
Cherie Case

Composition Services

Project Coordinator:
Patrick Redmond

Layout and Graphics:
Ana Carrillo, Erin Zeltner

Proofreader: Betty Kish

Publishing and Editorial for Technology Dummies

Richard Swadley, Vice President and Executive Group Publisher

Andy Cummings, Vice President and Publisher

Mary Bednarek, Executive Acquisitions Director

Mary C. Corder, Editorial Director

Publishing for Consumer Dummies

Kathleen Nebenhaus, Vice President and Executive Publisher

Composition Services

Debbie Stailey, Director of Composition Services

Table of Contents

Part VIII: Facebook on the Go ... 103

Part IX: Ten Frequently Asked Questions. 119

Introduction

*F*acebook connects you with the people you know and care about. It enables you to communicate, stay up-to-date, and keep in touch with friends and family anywhere. It facilitates your relationships online to help enhance them in person. Specifically, Facebook connects you with the *people* you know around *content* that is important to you. Whether you're the type to take photos or look at them, or write about your life, or read about your friends' lives, Facebook is designed to enable you to succeed. Maybe you like to share websites and news, play games, plan events, organize groups of people, or promote your business. Whatever you prefer, Facebook has you covered.

Facebook welcomes everyone: students and professionals; grandchildren (as long as they're at least age 13), parents, and grandparents; busy people; socialites; celebrities; distant friends; and roommates. No matter who you are, using Facebook can add value to your life.

About Facebook For Dummies

Facebook offers you control. Communication and information sharing are powerful only when you can do what you want within your comfort zone. Nearly every piece of information and means of connecting on Facebook comes with full privacy controls, allowing you to share and communicate exactly how — and with whom — you desire.

Facebook For Dummies, Pocket Edition is divided into nine parts:

- ✔ Part I of this book teaches you all the basics to get you up and running on Facebook. This information is more than enough for you to discover Facebook's value.

- ✔ Part II familiarizes you with the Timeline options and how to improve your Timeline.

- ✔ Part III details fast and easy ways to locate your friends on Facebook.

- ✔ Part IV gives you the lowdown on several cool ways to communicate with friends.

- ✔ Part V provides basic information about Facebook's many privacy and safety controls.

- ✔ Part VI shows how to upload and share photos, videos, and notes.

- ✔ Part VII helps you find the perfect Group to join and plan your next big Event.

- ✔ Part VIII shows you how to access and use Facebook Mobile, so you can stay connected anywhere, anytime.

- ✔ Part XI has ten frequently asked questions. It also has the answers.

Facebook regularly tweaks its pages, shuffling links to new places or renaming buttons. So don't be surprised if what you see on your computer screen doesn't exactly match what you see in this book. The look of Facebook may change, but the tools and functions tend to stay the same. If you get lost, be sure to visit Dummies.com for the latest news on Facebook's updates.

Conventions Used in This Book

In this book, we stick to a few conventions to help with readability. Whenever you have to type text, we show it in **bold**, so it's easy to see. Monofont text denotes an e-mail address or website URL. When you see an *italicized* word, look for its nearby definition. Facebook pages and features — such as the Friends box or the Privacy Overview page — are called out with capital letters. Numbered lists guide you through tasks that must be completed in order from top to bottom; bulleted lists can be read in any order you like (from top to bottom or bottom to top).

Finally, I, Carolyn, often state my opinions throughout this book. Though I have worked for Facebook in the past, the opinions expressed here represent only my perspective. I love Facebook and use it all the time, both before and after working there.

Icons Used in This Book

What's a *For Dummies* book without icons pointing you in the direction of great information that's sure to help you along your way? In this section, we briefly describe each icon we use in this book.

The Tip icon points out helpful information that is likely to improve your experience.

The Remember icon marks an interesting and useful fact — something that you may want to use later.

The Warning icon highlights lurking danger. With this icon, we're telling you to pay attention and proceed with caution.

Part I

Adding Your Own Face to Facebook

. . . .

In This Part

▶ Finding out what Facebook can do for you

▶ Signing up

▶ Creating your profile

▶ Getting Verified

. . . .

*T*hink about the people you interacted with throughout the past day. In the morning, you may have gone to get the paper and chatted with the neighbor. You may have asked your kids what time they'd be home and negotiated with your partner about whose turn it is to cook dinner. Perhaps you spent the day at the office, chatting, joking, and (heaven forbid) getting things done with your co-workers. In the evening, you may have shot off an e-mail to an old college roommate, called your mom (it's her birthday, after all), and made plans to have dinner with some friends this weekend. At the end of the day, you unwound in front of your favorite newscaster telling you about the various politicians and celebrities whose lives may (or may not) interest you. You may have, at various points in the day, asked someone to recommend a plumber to unclog your drain or had a full conversation of grunts with your dentist.

That's a one-foot view of the world in which you're the center.

Pan the camera back a ways (farther . . . farther . . . even farther), and you see that each person you interact with — family, friends, the newspaper delivery guy, the lunch lady, your favorite musician, and even me, your dedicated author — are at the center of their own realities. So is each person *they* know. The connections between every single person in the world intertwine, interplay, and interlock to form a sort of network. In the network of people you interact with — your friends, acquaintances, and loved ones — all these people exist online and represent themselves through Facebook, just like you're about to do. Facebook is the online representation of the web of connections between people in the real world. Facebook (and other Internet companies) like to call this network the *social graph.*

Now, you may be asking, if this graph or network exists in the real world, why do I need it online, too? Good question (gold stars all around). The answer is that having it online facilitates and improves all your social relationships. In other words, Facebook makes your life easier and your friendships better. It can help with the very practical, like remembering a friend's birthday, to the more abstract, like staying close with family you aren't physically near.

So . . . What Is Facebook, Exactly?

Yes, you're saying, I know it's going to help me stay in touch with my friends and communicate with the people in my life, but what *is* it?

Well, at its most basic, Facebook is a website. You'll find it through a web browser like Safari, Firefox, or

Internet Explorer, the same way you might navigate to a search engine like Google or to an airline's website to book tickets.

Facebook is a website where you go to accomplish certain tasks. These tasks usually fall under the umbrella category of *social maintenance*. For example, you may go to Facebook to

- ✔ Find the phone number of an old friend
- ✔ Check out what your friends are up to today
- ✔ Make a contact in a city you're moving to or at an office where you're applying for a job
- ✔ Plan an event
- ✔ Garner support for a cause
- ✔ Get recommendations from friends for movies, books, and restaurants
- ✔ Show off the pictures from your latest vacation
- ✔ Tell your friends and family about your recent successes, show them your photos, or let them know you're thinking of them
- ✔ Remember everyone's birthday

So what Facebook *is,* exactly, is a website built to help you represent yourself online and share with your real-world friends online. The rest of it — how that's accomplished, what people typically share on Facebook, and how it all works — is what this book is all about.

Discovering What You Can Do on Facebook

Now that you know that Facebook is a means by which you can connect with people who matter to

you, your next question may be, "How?" More gold
stars for you! In the next few sections, we give you an
overview.

✔ **Establish a Timeline:** If you want people to
know even more about you, you can add histori-
cal events that are significant in your life: times
you moved, or got a new pet, or a new job, or
got engaged. Then your friends can scroll back
through time to see everything that's important
to you.

You show different slices of your life and per-
sonality to different people, and your Facebook
Timeline allows you to do the same.

To this end, your Timeline is set up with all
kinds of privacy controls to specify *who* you
want to see *which* information. We discuss privacy further in Part V.

✔ **Connect with friends:** Now that you know about
Timelines, you should know that there are ways
to connect your Timeline to the Timelines of
people you know. These connections are called
friendships. On Facebook, it's pretty common to
refer to *friending* people you know. This just
means establishing the virtual connection.
Friending people allows you to communicate
and share with them more easily.

After you find a few people, use those connections to find other people you know by searching through their friends for familiar names. We
explain how to find people you know on
Facebook in Part III.

✔ **Communicate with Facebook friends:** Facebook
streamlines finding and contacting people in a
reliable forum. If the friend you're reaching out

to is active on Facebook, no matter where she lives or how many times she's changed her e-mail address, you can reach one another.

✓ **Share your thoughts:** All day long, things are happening to all of us that make us just want to turn to our friends and say, "You know what? . . . That's what." Facebook gives you the stage and an eager audience. In Part IV, we explain how you can make short or long posts about the things happening around you, and how they're distributed to your friends in an easy way.

✓ **Share your pictures:** Facebook provides one easy-to-access location for all your photos. Every photo you upload can be linked to the Profiles of the people in the photo. Facebook gives you the power to control exactly who has access to your photos.

✓ **Plan Events, join groups:** Facebook is meant to facilitate interactions when face time isn't possible or to facilitate the planning of face time. Two of the greatest tools for this are Facebook Events and Facebook Groups.

✓ **Facebook and the web:** After you get a little more comfortable with the Facebook basics, you can try some of the thousands of applications and websites that allow you to interact with your Facebook friends through their services.

✓ **Promote a cause or business:** If you're the one managing something like a small business, a cause, or a newsletter, you can also create a Page. After you've created that page, your users/customers/fans can like it and then you can update them with news about whatever's going on in the world of your store/cause/thing.

Keeping in Mind What You Can't Do on Facebook

Facebook is meant to represent real people and real associations; it's also meant to be safe. Many of the rules of participation on Facebook exist to uphold those two goals.

Note: There are things you can't do on Facebook other than what we list here. For example, you can't send multiple unsolicited messages to people you're not friends with, you can't join the school network of a school you didn't attend (or a workplace network of a company you don't work for), and you can't spin straw into gold. These rules may change how you use Facebook, but probably won't change *whether* you use it. The following four rules are highlighted in this section because, if any are a problem for you, you probably won't get to the rest of the book.

- ✔ **You can't lie:** Okay, you can, but you shouldn't, especially not about your basic information. Lying about your identity is a violation of the Statement of Rights and Responsibilities and grounds for your Profile being disabled. Although many people try, Facebook doesn't let anyone sign up with an obviously fake name like Marilyn Manson or Fakey McFakerson. Those who do make it past the name checks will likely find their account flagged and disabled.

- ✔ **You can't be twelve:** Or younger. Seriously. Facebook takes very seriously the U.S. law that prohibits minors under the age of 13 from creating an online Profile for themselves. This rule is in place for the safety of minors, and it's a particular safety rule that Facebook takes extremely seriously. If you or someone you know on

Facebook is under 13, deactivate (or make them deactivate) the account now. If you're reported to the Facebook user operations team and they confirm that you are underage, your account will be disabled.

✔ **You can't troll or spam:** On the Internet, *trolling* refers to posting deliberately offensive material to websites in order to get people upset. *Spamming* refers to sending out bulk promotional messages. If you do either of these things on Facebook, there's a good chance your account will be shut down.

The logic for this is that Facebook is about real people and real connections. It is one thing to message a mutual friend or the occasional stranger whose Timeline implies being open to meeting new people if the two of you have matching interests. However, between Facebook's automatic detection systems and user-generated reports, sending too many unsolicited messages is likely to get your account flagged and disabled.

✔ **You can't upload illegal content:** Facebook Users live in virtually every country in the world, so Facebook is often obligated to respect the local laws for its users. Respecting these laws is something Facebook has to do regardless of its own position on pornography, copyrighted material, hate speech, depictions of crimes, and other offensive content. However, doing so is also in line with Facebook's value of being a safe, happy place for people 13 and older. Don't confuse this with censorship; Facebook is all about freedom of speech and self-expression, but the moment that compromises anyone's safety or breaks any law, disciplinary action is taken.

Realizing How Facebook Is Different from Other Social Sites

Several social sites besides Facebook try to help people connect.

In some cases, these sites have slightly different goals than Facebook. LinkedIn, for example, is a tool for connecting with people specifically for career networking. Match.com (www.match.com) is a social networking site specifically geared toward people looking to date. Alternatively, other sites have the same goals as Facebook; they just have different strategies. MySpace gives users complete customization over the look and feel of their Profile, whereas Facebook maintains a pretty consistent design and expects users to differentiate their Profiles by uploading unique content. On the other extreme, Twitter allows its members to share very short bits of text and photos to achieve super-simple and consistent information sharing, whereas Facebook allows more flexibility with respect to sharing complete photo albums, videos, and more. That's not to say one model is better than another; different models may appeal to different people.

Signing Up for Facebook

Officially, all you need to join Facebook is a valid e-mail address. Figure 1-1 shows the crucial part of the sign-up page, which you can find by navigating to www.facebook.com. As you can see, you need to fill out a few things:

- **First and Last Name**
- **E-mail**
- **Password**

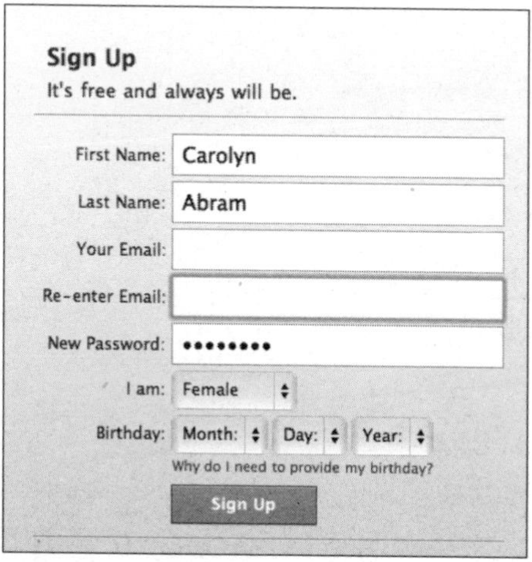

Figure 1-1: Enter information here to create a Facebook account.

✔ **Sex (I am).** If you want to hide your gender on your Profile, you'll be able to do so after you sign up.

✔ **Birthday.** You'll be able to hide this information on your Profile later.

✔ **Security Check (shown in Figure 1-2).** Asking you to type the word in a CAPTCHA is Facebook's way of making sure you're a real person, not a spam-producing computer or robot. You see the CAPTCHA after filling out your information and clicking Sign Up.

After you've filled out this information, click Sign Up (that's the big green button). Congratulations: You have officially joined Facebook!

Sign Up
It's free and always will be.

Security Check

NQBU

Can't read the text above?
Try another text; or an audio captcha

Text in the box: [   ]   What's this?

◄ Back   [Sign Up]

By clicking Sign Up, you are indicating that you have read and agree to the Terms of Use and Privacy Policy.

Figure 1-2: Security checks weed out robots.

When you click Sign Up, you are agreeing to Facebook's Statement of Rights and Responsibilities and Privacy Policy. Most websites have fairly similar Terms and Policies, but if you're curious about just what Facebook's say, you can always follow the links at the bottom of every Facebook page.

Getting Started

Facebook puts all its users through a three-step Getting Started Wizard to help start them out on the right foot. This is one of those places where what we think you should do and what Facebook thinks you should do line up exactly, so I'll go through all three of these steps: what to enter as well as why they are important to using Facebook.

Step 1: Find Friends

The Find Friends step is first because it is that important to enjoying Facebook.

You have many ways to find friends on Facebook. We cover them in Part III, as well as talk more about what friendship really means on Facebook.

Step 2: Information

While you're getting started, Facebook asks for only a little bit of Information, the part that we like to call the *bio*. Facebook asks for this bio because this is the information that will help your friends find you. It will also appear on your Timeline.

Facebook asks for three fields. You can fill out all or none of them, but we definitely recommend filling them all out:

- ✔ **High School:** Enter the high school you attended and your class year. Just enter one for now; you'll be able to add more schools later.

- ✔ **College/University:** If you attended college, enter your school and class year. If you attended more than one school because you transferred or attended a graduate program, just pick one school for now. You'll be able to add the rest later.

- ✔ **Employer:** Enter the name of the company you work for. For now, enter wherever you are currently working or where you worked most recently. You'll be able to enter a full work history later on.

Now that you've entered this information, you've made it easier for old friends to find and identify you. If you have a common name, this is especially important.

Step 3: Profile picture

To add your Profile picture, make sure you have a photo you want to use saved somewhere on your computer's hard drive, and follow these steps:

1. **Click Upload a Photo.**
2. **Click Choose File.**
3. **Select your desired photo and click Select or OK.**
4. **Click Save & Continue.**

Here are a few quick tips on selecting a Profile picture:

- ✔ **Make a good first impression.** What picture represents you?

- ✔ **Consider who will see your Profile picture.** By default, your Profile picture appears in search results that are visible to all of Facebook and can even be made available to the larger Internet population.

- ✔ **Remember that you're not stuck with it.** Keep in mind that you can easily change your Profile picture at any time.

Well, that's pretty much the basics of getting started on Facebook. We hope by now you've added a few friends, some information about yourself, and a Profile picture.

Trust Me: Getting Confirmed and Verified

Facebook is a website for real identity and real people. To protect this idea, Facebook has systems in place to detect any fake Profiles. Fake Profiles may be jokes (for example, someone creating a Profile for her dog), or they may be *spammers* (robots creating accounts to send thousands of fake friend requests). Regardless, they're not allowed on the site.

Confirmation

Confirmation is Facebook's way of trying to make sure you are really you, and that the e-mail address you used to sign up is really yours. To confirm that you are, in fact, you; and that the e-mail address is, in fact, yours, go to your e-mail, look for that message, and open it. (It will usually have a subject like "Just one more step to get started on Facebook" or "Facebook Confirmation.") That e-mail contains a link. Click the link in that e-mail and you will be confirmed.

 You may have already confirmed your e-mail address by using the Friend Finder or other normal activities. If Facebook isn't bugging you about it with banners or follow up e-mails, you can pretty much assume you're good to go.

Verification

Verification is a way to make sure that beyond just owning an e-mail account (which, unfortunately, any evil robot can do), you are a real human being who won't abuse Facebook or post inappropriate content.

If you're concerned about being verified right away, you can be verified by activating Facebook Mobile:

1. **Go to the Mobile Settings page by directing your browser to the following link:** `www.facebook.com/settings?tab=mobile`.

2. **Click the green Add Your Phone Number button.**

3. **Enter your password into the dialog box that appears.**

   Enter your Facebook password, not your phone's password.

4. **Select your country and mobile carrier.**

5. **Click Next.**

6. **Now pick up your phone. Use it to text the letter F to 32665.**

   Facebook texts back a confirmation code.

7. **Back at your computer, enter that code into the designated box onscreen and click Confirm.**

   After you've confirmed this code, your account is verified.

Part II

Building Out Your Timeline

*T*he latest iteration of Facebook gathers your profile information into a format called the timeline. Your Facebook timeline is more than just a bunch of information — it's an ongoing, ever-evolving story about you. Did you ever have to respond to a writing prompt that asked you to write page 73 of your 248-page autobiography? Your timeline is the page you are working on right now, except your autobiography is a complete multimedia presentation, pulling together your words, your photos, your friends' thoughts, and your postings. All of those things together tell the reader both who you are and what's important to you. Your Facebook timeline is not about altering who you are but rather representing yourself. Use it to introduce and share yourself with the people who matter to you. Use it to construct and take note of the important events in your life. What do you want people to know about you? What do you want your friends to find out about you?

The timeline, shown in Figure 2-1, has a few different portions: the at-a-glance section running across the bulk of the screen at the top of the page, the navigational markers to the very right of this, the Share menu or Publisher just below, and the timeline itself, extending from the present back and back and back to the day you were born.

Figure 2-1: A timeline.

Navigating the Timeline

In this section, we walk you through the parts of the timeline.

  ✔ **Photos:** The first impression of any timeline, including your own, is the two photos that greet you when you first arrive. The big background one is called the *cover photo*. It's meant to be sort of like the cover of a music album. It can be anything you choose. The second, smaller photo is meant to be more like a headshot, your actual *profile* *photo.* This smaller photo appears on Facebook anywhere your name is: places you comment on posts or where your posts are shared.

✔ **At-a-Glance Info:** This section includes your Name, info about where you work and live, where you went to school, and who you're in a relationship with (assuming you choose to share these facts).

✔ **The Share menu:** This is what you use to post content such as statuses, photos, and more to your timeline (and to your friends' News Feeds). It's also how you add events to your timeline that you want to commemorate.

✔ **The thin blue line:** Scrolling down reveals an extended blue line that starts in the present, and if you keep scrolling, it goes all the way back to your birth. At various points in time, bullets call out significant events, statuses, photos, or actions you took on Facebook.

✔ **Jumping around in time:** To the right of your cover photo is a condensed timeline, which allows you to jump to any point in time you wish to see just by clicking it.

Cover Me

The two photos at the top of your Profile make the initial first impression to all visitors to your Profile. The cover photo is the larger photo that serves as a background to your Profile. People often choose visually striking photos or images that really speak to who they are and what they love — you'll see a lot of nature shots. To change your cover photo, follow these steps:

1. **Hover over your existing cover photo.**
2. **Click the Change Cover button.**

This opens the Change Cover menu, which has four options: Choose from Photos, Upload Photo, Reposition, and Remove.

3. **Click Choose from Photos to select a cover photo from photos you've already added to Facebook.**

3a. **Choose Upload Photo to select a cover photo from your computer.**

4. **Select your cover photo by clicking your desired album and then the desired photo within that album.**

   This brings you back to your timeline, where you should see the new cover photo in place with an overlaid message, "Drag to Reposition Cover."

4a. **Select the photo file you want as your cover and click Open.**

   This brings you back to your timeline, where you should see the new cover photo in place with an overlaid message: Drag to Reposition Cover.

5. **Click and drag your cover photo to position it correctly within the frame of the screen.**

6. **Click Save Changes.**

   Your new cover photo is now in place.

Much like your cover photo, you can change your profile picture as often as you choose. All the photos you make into your profile picture are automatically added to the "Profile Pictures" album.

All About Me

The at-a-glance box gives you (and your friends) what I like to think of as the dinner party basics: where you live, what you do, where you're from, whom you're with. But clicking the About link opens the About section of your timeline.

This page houses lots of information about you in a few boxes: Work and Education, Basic Info, Living, Relationships and Family, Contact Info. You can visit the About section to edit this information as well as edit who can see it. In general, you have five basic privacy options to remember:

✔ **Public or Everyone:** This means that anyone who finds your timeline, potentially anywhere on the Internet, can see this piece of information. This is a good setting for the things that are not very personal or are already public knowledge.

✔ **Friends:** This means that only your friends can see that piece of information. This setting is useful for more personal things like your contact information.

✔ **Friends Except Acquaintances:** This option refers to the "acquaintances" smart list that Facebook creates for many users. People who have been added to this list will be unable to see this information.

✔ **Only Me:** This option allows you to keep information on your profile for your own reference, but not show it to anyone else on Facebook. This is useful for information that Facebook requires from you, like your gender or birthday, but that you don't want to share more widely.

✔ **Custom:** You can use custom settings to show items to specific groups of people. You can choose a setting like Friends of Friends if you want something to be visible to more than just friends, but not to the public; or you can even choose to show something only to specific friends, or to hide it from specific friends. To learn about these privacy options and how to use them, check out Part V.

All information fields in the About section are optional to fill out. If something doesn't apply to you, or you don't want to share that information, just leave it blank.

Basic Information

Your Basic Information is just what it sounds like: the very basics about you that you might use to identify who you are and where you're from. Click Edit to open a pop-up screen to edit any of these fields and who can see them.

- ✔ **Sex (I Am):** You entered your sex when you signed up for Facebook, and Facebook mirrors your selection here. If you don't want people to see your sex on your timeline, you can deselect the check box opposite this field.

- ✔ **Birthday:** You also entered your birthday when you registered for Facebook. Here, you have the ability to tweak the date (in case you messed up) as well as decide what people can see about your birthday. Some people don't like sharing their age, their birthday, or both. If you're one of these people, use this drop-down menu to select what you want to share.

- ✔ **Interested In:** This field is primarily used by people to signal their sexual orientation. Some people feel that this section makes Facebook seem like a dating site, so if that doesn't sound like you, you don't have to fill it out.

- ✔ **Languages:** Languages might seem a little less basic than, say, your city, but you can enter any languages you speak here.

- ✔ **Religion:** You can choose to list your religion and describe it.

✔ **Political Views:** You can also choose to list your political views and further explain them with a description.

 Whenever you edit a section of your information, click Save (a button at the bottom of the page) so you don't lose your work.

Contact Information

Privacy settings are a very useful part of Facebook because people can share their telephone numbers, e-mail addresses, and other contact information without the whole world seeing it. This enables incredibly useful features (such as Facebook Mobile — see Part VIII) and the ability to track down someone's e-mail address and phone number — even if you were accidentally left off his "I'm moving/changing jobs/changing names" e-mail. For your own contact information, share what you're comfortable sharing and try to keep it up-to-date. I talk more about the privacy settings that protect this information in Part V.

 If you are editing information as you go, remember to click the blue Save buttons after you make changes on each page. Otherwise, all your hard work will be undone.

Part III

Finding Facebook Friends

*H*undreds of sayings abound about friendship and friends, and most of them can be boiled down into one catch-all adage: friends, good; no friends, bad. This is true in life and it's true on Facebook. Without your friends on Facebook, you find yourself at some point looking at a blank screen and asking, "Okay, now what?" With friends, you find yourself at some point looking at photos of a high school reunion and asking, "Oh, dear. How did that last hour go by so quickly?"

Most of Facebook's functionality is built around the premise that you have a certain amount of information that you want your friends to see (and maybe some information that you don't want *all* your friends to see, but that's what privacy settings are for). So, if you don't have friends who are seeing your Timeline, what's the point in creating one? Messages aren't that useful unless you send them to someone. Photos are made to be viewed, but if the access is limited to friends, well, you need to find some friends.

On Facebook, in general, friendships are *reciprocal,* which means if you add someone as a friend, they have to confirm the friendship before it appears on both timelines. If someone adds you as a friend, you can choose between Confirm and Not Now. If you confirm the friend, congrats: You have a new friend! And if you ignore the friend, the other person won't be informed.

What Is a Facebook Friend?

Good question. In many ways, a *Facebook friend* is the same as a real-life friend (although, to quote many people I know, "You're not real friends unless you're Facebook friends"). These are the people you hang out with, keep in touch with, care about, and want to publicly acknowledge as a friend. These usually aren't people you met on Facebook; rather they're the people you call on the phone; stop and catch up with if you cross paths at the grocery; or invite over for parties, dinners, and general social gatherings.

In real life, there are many shades of friendship — think of the differences between acquaintances, a friend from work, an activity buddy, and best friends. Facebook gives you a few tools for negotiating these levels of friendship, which we cover in this chapter, but by default, most friendships are lumped into a blanket category of "friend."

So here's what happens, by default, in a Facebook friendship.

> ✔ **They can see your posts and other information on your timeline.** Remember, this is what happens by default. You can actually control which friends can see which posts more specifically by learning about your privacy options (which you

learning about your privacy options (which you can do in Part V), and about Friend Lists, which we go over later in this chapter.

✔ **They also see new posts in their News Feeds and Tickers on their Home page.** Again, the information your friends see in their News Feeds and Tickers depends on the audience you've chosen to share each post with. Friends (or subscribers) can see only posts you've published to that audience.

✔ **You can see their posts and other information on their timeline.** This, of course, depends on their own privacy settings, but in general, you'll be able to see more as a friend than you did before you became friends.

✔ **You also see new posts from them in your News Feed and Ticker on your Home page.** This depends on your friend's sharing settings, but more importantly, you can control whose posts you see in your News Feed and Ticker through managing your *subscriptions*. Subscribing to someone's posts is similar to subscribing to a daily newspaper: their posts show up every day on your front stoop . . . er, Home page. Like a very advanced newspaper subscription, you can control how much you see about any one person, and even choose certain types of posts you want to see. You can also fully unsubscribe from someone's posts while remaining friends with them.

✔ **You'll be listed as friends on one another's timeline.** This is a small detail, but it's important in understanding the difference between becoming friends with someone and simply subscribing to someone's posts. Lots of people, especially public figures or people who have a business of some sort, allow you to subscribe to their posts without becoming friends. In these cases, you see their posts on your Home page, but they won't see your posts unless they choose to subscribe to you.

If Only Real Life Had a Friend Finder

Friend Finder is a tool that matches e-mail addresses from your e-mail address book to people's timelines on Facebook. Because each e-mail address can be associated with only one Facebook account, you can count on your matches finding the right people whom you already know through e-mail. With your permission, Friend Finder also invites those people who don't have a Facebook account that matches the e-mail in your address book to join Facebook. If they join based on an invite you send, they find a Friend Request from you waiting when they join.

To use Friend Finder, you need to give Facebook your e-mail address and e-mail password. Facebook doesn't store this information: It just uses it to retrieve your contacts list that one time.

The following steps make several assumptions, namely, that you use web-based e-mail (Hotmail, Gmail, Yahoo! Mail, and so on), that you haven't used Friend Finder recently, and that the address book for the e-mail has a bunch of your friends in it. Here's how to use Friend Finder:

1. **Click the Friends icon next to the word *Facebook* on the big blue bar on top.**

   This opens the Friend Request menu.

2. **At the top-right corner of the menu, click the Find Friends link.**

   Figure 3-1 shows the Friend Finder.

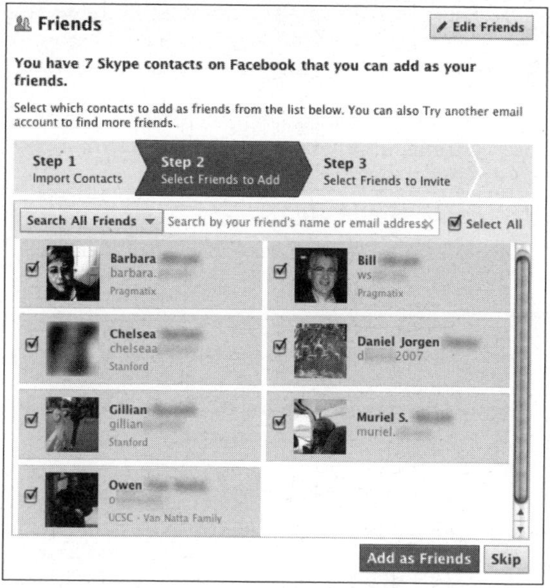

Figure 3-1: The Friend Selector portion of Friend Finder.

3. **Select the e-mail or instant message service you use.**

   This may be Windows Live Hotmail, AOL, or any number of other e-mail services.

4. **Enter your e-mail address into the Your Email field.**

5. **Enter your e-mail password (not your Facebook password) into the Email Password box and then click Find Friends.**

These instructions are meant for first-time users
of the Friend Finder. If you've used it before, or if
you're currently logged into your webmail client,
you may see some fields prefilled or additional
pop-up prompts asking you for your permission
to send information to Facebook. Don't worry if it
doesn't match the figures here at the beginning.

6. Decide whether to

- *Add everyone as a friend.* Click Add as Friends.

- *Not friend anyone.* Click Skip.

- *Add many people as a friend.* Click the faces
  or check boxes to the left of the specific
  names that you don't want to be friends with.
  After you deselect all the people you don't
  want, click Add as Friends.

- *Add a few people as friends.* Uncheck the
  Select All box at the top of the screen. Then,
  check the box to the left of the name or click
  the face of anyone you want to add as a
  friend. When you've selected everyone you'd
  like to invite, click Add as Friends.

**7. (Optional) Invite people to join Facebook and
become your friend.**

Similar to adding friends, you can

- *Invite all these contacts.* Click Invite to Join.

- *Invite none of these contacts.* Click Skip.

- *Invite some of these contacts.* Select the Invite
  Some Friends option and then use the check
  boxes to the left of their e-mail addresses to
  choose which ones you want to Invite to join
  Facebook.

When you've made your selections, click Send
Invites or Invite to Join. If you don't want to send
any invitations, click Skip.

After taking all these steps, I hope you manage to send a few Friend Requests. Your friends need to confirm your requests before you officially become friends on Facebook, so you may not be able to see your friends' full Timelines until that confirmation happens.

Find Classmates and Co-workers

Friend Finder works by looking for large groups of people you might want to become friends with. A common assumption is that you'll want to become friends with people you've gone to school with and worked with over the years. To find these people, follow these steps:

1. **Click the Friends icon next to the word *Facebook* on the big blue bar on top.**

   This opens a little menu.

2. **At the top of the menu, click the Find Friends link.**

   This brings you to the Friend Finder page.

3. **Click Other Tools (usually the bottom option).**

   This expands a menu of possibilities based on information you have filled out on your timeline.

4. **Click any of the Find Coworkers From or Find Classmates From links.**

   All these links go to the same place, which is a page for browsing people on Facebook shown in Figure 3-2.

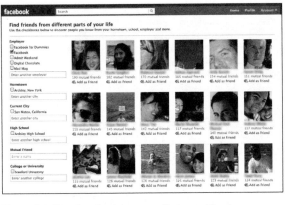

Figure 3-2: Use the check boxes to find your friends.

5. **Use the check boxes on the left side of the page to look for people from your various jobs or schools.**

   Selecting a check box displays people from that school or company. You can also look for people from your hometown, current city, or workplace by entering a mutual friend's name.

When you check more than one box, it actually shows you *fewer* people because now Facebook is looking for people who both worked at Mom's Pizza *and* went to Hamilton High School. To find more people, check only one box at a time.

You can actually browse for people in cities, companies, and colleges other than the ones you've listed on your timeline. Look for the empty boxes that say Add Another and type in the school, city, or company where you think you know people.

Creating Your Own Friend Lists

Lists (capital L) are subsets of your giant list of friends (lowercase l). Confused yet? Friend Lists are a way of organizing your friends into lists to make your Facebook experience even easier and more personalized to you and your types of friends.

To create a Friend List, follow these steps:

1. **Hover on the Friends section of the left menu on the Home page and click the More link that appears.**

   This brings you to a list of all your Lists.

2. **Click the Create a List button in the upper-right corner.**

3. **In the window that opens, type the name of your list.**

4. **Select friends who belong on this list by typing their names into the Members box.**

   Facebook will attempt to autocomplete the name as you type. After you see your friend's face, click or hit enter to select her.

5. **Click Create List.**

   Now, wherever Friend Lists appear on Facebook, including where you set privacy, Chat, the Inbox, and the Friends page, you have access to the new list you just created. It also appears on the left side of the Edit Friends page.

You can always edit the name or membership of a list later by selecting the list name from the tab on the left of the Friends page. From there, you can change the name, or delete or add members. Also, whenever viewing friends on the Manage Friends page, you can add them to lists by selecting the Add to List drop-down menu to the right of their names.

Even if you don't create your own Lists, you may notice that Lists appear in the Friends section of your left-hand menu. These lists are created automatically by Facebook based on information it has about you and your friends. For example, you may notice a list named after your high school or after your workplace. If people have listed themselves as your family members, they may be added to your family list. Other lists, like Close Friends, change over time as you interact more with certain people, and less with others. You can still edit these lists in case Facebook made a mistake.

Discovering the Facebook Friend Philosophy

You might hear different reports on the rules for Facebook. You might hear that it's rude to ignore a friend request. Pay no attention to these ugly rumors. The truth about Facebook Friend etiquette is here.

Choose your friends wisely

Generally, you send Friend Requests to and confirm Friend Requests from only people you actually know. If you don't know them — *random Friend Requests* — click Not Now. For all the reasons enumerated in the preceding section — your privacy, News Feed, and reflection of reality — don't declare friendship unless some kind of relationship actually exists. Remember the lecture you got about choosing good friends when you were in high school? It's every bit as true now.

It's quality, not quantity

Another common misperception about Facebook is
that it's all about the race to get the most friends.
This is very, very wrong. Between the News Feed and
privacy implications of friendship, I always aim to keep
my Friend List to the people I actually care about. Now,
the number of people you care about — including the
people you care about the most and those you care
about least — may be large or small. The average
number of friends that a person has on Facebook is
around 120. Does a person with 120 friends care about
them all equally? Probably not. Does this mean that
person is shallow? No. It means that this person is
keeping up with and keeping track of all the friends
who have come and gone through a lifetime. Changing
jobs, schools, and locations also comes with new
friends, but that doesn't displace the fact that you care
about friends from your past.

Should you aim to have 120 friends? No. Some folks
have a great Facebook experience with fewer than
30 friends. With that number, they can share photos
with friends, play games with people, and have a
pretty active News Feed. Aim to have all the people
you care about on your Friend List. Maybe that's a big
number, or maybe it's a small number; the part that
counts is that you want to see them in the list, smiling
back at you.

Part IV

Keeping Up with Your Friends

- -

In This Part

▶ Messaging your friends

▶ Sharing interesting content from the Web

▶ Communicating openly

- -

*C*hances are you communicate with other people online. You may use e-mail all the time, or use instant messaging programs like AIM or Skype. If you have a smartphone, you probably check e-mail and text messages on it as well. This part explains some modes of communication on Facebook.

Just between You and Me

Facebook stitches together e-mail, texting, and instant messaging with a Facebook twist.

Messages

With Facebook's messaging system, you no longer have to remember e-mail addresses, screen names, or handles. You just have to remember people's names. Figure 4-1 shows the most basic New Message dialog box. I generated this one by going to the Messages Inbox and clicking the New Message button.

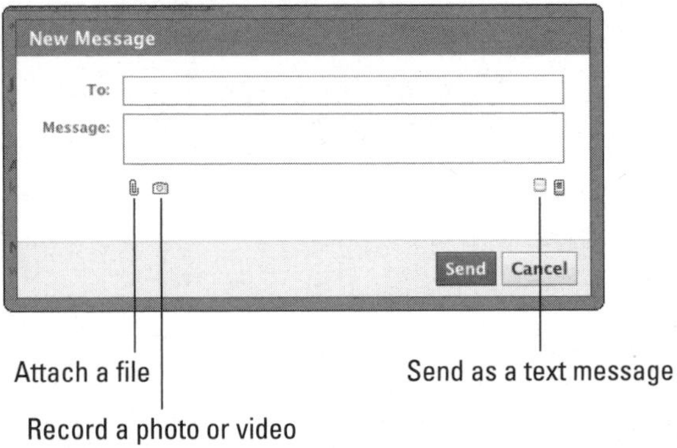

New Message
To:
Message:
Send
Cancel
Attach a file
Send as a text message
Record a photo or video

Figure 4-1: Send a new message.

This dialog box has only two fields for you to fill out: a To field and a message box where you type the text of your message. If you're used to using e-mail, this may strike you as a little odd because it doesn't have a cc, bcc, or subject line.

To address your message, simply start typing the name of the person you are messaging into the To field. Facebook auto-completes with the names of your friends as you type. When you see the name you want, highlight it and click or press Enter.

Here are other things you might want to know about Facebook messages:

- **Messaging multiple people at one time:** You can type more than one name if you want, and you can type the name of a Group you belong to or a Friend List you have created.

✔ **Message threads:** On Facebook, the series of messages between two people is called a *conversation* or *thread*. This is because when you look at a message, it doesn't stand alone; rather, it is added to the bottom of all the messages, chats, and texts you have ever sent each other through Facebook.

✔ **Messaging e-mail addresses:** You can send a message to someone's e-mail address if he isn't yet on Facebook. Simply type the full e-mail address. Separate multiple e-mail addresses with commas or semicolons.

✔ **Messaging non-friends:** You can message people you aren't friends with on Facebook, but not from a blank message box. Instead, search for the person you want to message, and click Send Message from their Timeline or search result.

Sharing

Facebook has a specific Share feature, designed to make it easy to post and send content that you find both on Facebook and on the web. Perhaps you've already noticed the little Share links all over Facebook. They show up on albums, links, individual photos, notes, events, groups, News Feed stories, and more. They help you share content quickly without having to copy and paste.

The Share box gives you five options for sharing. You can share

✔ **On your own timeline:** This option posts the content to your timeline the same way you would post a link or a photo from your Share

menu. This means it will go into your friends'
News Feeds as well.

✔ **On a friend's timeline:** This option is the same
as copying and pasting a link into a timeline
post you leave on your friend's timeline (but it's
much easier than all that copy/paste nonsense).

✔ **In a group:** This option allows you to post the
content to a group you are a member of. You can
learn more about sharing with groups in Part VII.

✔ **On your Page** (for Page owners only): Pages
don't have timelines yet, but if you are the
admin of a Page — a Profile for non-people —
you can share things as a post from your Page.

✔ **In a private Message:** This accomplishes the
same thing as copying and pasting a link into a
message to a friend. In other words, only the
friend you send it to will see the link, whereas
sharing via the timeline means anyone viewing
your friend's timeline can also see the link.
Messages are talked about in Part VIII.

After you've chosen how you want to share the item,
you can write something about what you're sharing. If
you are sharing an article, you can edit the preview
that appears in the post. The Share box shows you
the preview, and you can hover over the headline and
teaser text to highlight them. Click the highlighted
text to begin editing the preview. You can also choose
a thumbnail to accompany most shared links. Use the
arrow keys next to the words Choose a Thumbnail to
see your options. If you don't like any of them, check
the No Thumbnail box.

Chat

Sometimes you've got something to say to someone,
and you've got to say it now. If that someone is not
sitting right next to you, try sending her an instant

message through Facebook Chat. Chat allows you to see which friends are online at the same time you are, and then enables you to send quick messages back and forth with any one of those people, or have multiple simultaneous conversations with different friends.

 Facebook doesn't discriminate when it comes to the way you talk to your friends. Whether a message or a chat, it all goes into your conversation history in your Messages Inbox.

You'll find Chat in the bottom-right corner of any page on Facebook. When a friend sends you a chat, a small window pops up next to the Chat bar in the bottom right of your screen. To send a chat message back to them, simply click into the text field at the bottom of the chat window, start typing, and press Enter when you're done. Your message appears below your friend's, just as it does with most IM services.

To start a new chat with someone, you just need to select his or her name from the Chat menu. This opens a chat window that you can type in.

By default, the Chat menu displays the friends you message and chat with most often, in alphabetical order. A green dot next to their name means they are active on Facebook, as shown in Figure 4-2. A blue crescent moon means they are logged in but aren't currently active. No icon means they aren't currently logged in.

Poke

On Friends' Profiles, you see a Poke option in the drop-down option of the Gear button (next to the Message button). Since Facebook began, the most common question I've heard is, "What's a Poke?" We can tell you what it does, but we can't tell you what it is; it can mean something different to everyone. In

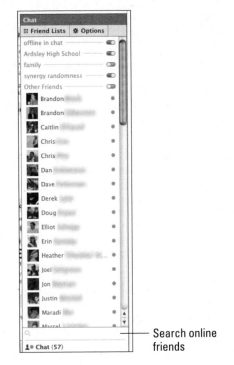

Search online
friends

Figure 4-2: The Chat menu.

some cases, Poke is a form of flirtation. Other times, Poke may mean a genuine thinking-of-you. Some people do it just to say, "Hi."

Public Displays of Affection

Facebook encourages openness by the way it allows more information to flow to more people, which deepens and strengthens relationships. Two ways to communicate publicly are through the Timeline and by commenting, but there are many other ways to keep in touch and share information, as well.

Common story types

Here are some of the common story types you might encounter:

- ✔ **Status Updates:** Status updates are the short little posts that your friends make about what's going on in their lives.

- ✔ **Links:** Figure 4-3 shows a post sharing a link. One of the chief ways I get my news: Friends share links to articles, and the previews are so interesting that I have to read the whole article. Click the links (or the article's title) to go to the articles.

- ✔ **Photos:** Figure 4-4 shows a post about photos. When people add photos or are tagged in photos, it creates this type of post, with information about who was tagged and a sample of the photos that were added. Click the photos to see bigger versions and browse the entire album.

- ✔ **Videos:** In a video story, clicking the Play button on the preview expands the story to show a play-ing card–sized version of the video. Clicking the title of the video will take you to the video's page, which may be on Facebook (if your friend used Facebook to add the video) or another video site like YouTube (if your friend used another video site and posted the link to Facebook).

Figure 4-3: Use your status to share links to articles.

Figure 4-4: Photo stories.

✔ **Timeline Posts:** Figure 4-5 shows a timeline post story between two friends. The first person wrote the message on the second person's timeline.

 You see timeline post stories only when you are friends with both of the people involved. You won't see stories about a friend posting on a non-friend's timeline.

✔ **Check-ins/Check-in tags:** A check-in is something that you can do from either your mobile phone or the share menu on News Feed or timeline. It allows you (or your friends) to use GPS to mark, on Facebook, where you are. Check-ins are often accompanied by mobile photo uploads or status updates.

Amy Karasavas ▶ Erin
You can certainly be the Chevy to my Paul! Your blazer collection is about to
come in handy.
Like · Comment · See Friendship · 2 minutes ago · 🔝

Figure 4-5: A timeline post between friends.

- ✔ **Likes:** Like stories are usually just quick little stories that let you know what Pages your friends have Liked recently. The Pages are linked so you can click right through to check them out yourself.

- ✔ **Read/Watch/Listen:** Certain services and websites, such as the music site Spotify, may prompt you to grant blanket permission to automatically post specific actions you take on their site to Facebook.

- ✔ **Friendships:** Friendship stories might be about just two people becoming friends or about one person becoming friends with lots of different people.

- ✔ **Changed Timeline Pictures:** Timeline picture stories are simply about your friends' new timeline pictures. Click through to look at the full-sized ones; the preview can be tiny!

- ✔ **Events:** Stories about events (usually letting you know which friends have RSVPed *yes* to an event) include a link to the event, so if you're looking for somewhere to go, you can say *yes,* too.

Talking through Timeline

Timelines wind up being one of the places you are most likely to reach out to a friend. Usually leaving a timeline post or a message that is visible on a timeline is a way of tapping a friend on the shoulder to remind him you're there. Sometimes people have entire conversations on each other's timelines.

To post on your friend's timeline, follow these steps:

1. **Go to his timeline.**

   Unless he has changed his privacy settings, he has a Share menu (previously known as the Publisher) at the top of his timeline, just like you have in yours.

2. **Click the type of post you want to leave.**

   You can post just text by clicking into the text box that says What's on Your Mind? Click Photo to post a photo or video.

3. **Type your comment to your friend.**

4. **When you're done, click Post.**

If you are choosing to share on your own timeline, you can click the drop-down menu to set privacy on the post.

 Unlike the posts that you write for your own timeline, you don't have specific privacy controls on the timeline posts you leave for friends. They may be seen by mutual friends (in their News Feeds), or by someone visiting your friend's timeline. If you're worried about who's going to see what you're writing, you may be better off sending a private message.

 Although there aren't any rules around when you can or can't post on someone's timeline, one convention that has evolved over time is the Happy Birthday timeline post. Because people are reminded of birthdays on Facebook, it's easy to pop on over to your friend's timeline and write a quick "Happy Birthday!" in honor of their day. It makes for a sweet day on the receiving end as well.

Comments and Likes

In addition to leaving a timeline post, you can interact with your friends on Facebook by commenting or liking the things they post. Frequently, people post things that you want to respond to. You may read an article they posted and want to respond to the viewpoint with one of your own. Their photos may be so beautiful that you just have to tell them. Or, you may just need to point out something they hadn't considered.

To comment on anything on Facebook, follow these steps:

1. **Click Comment.**

   This expands the comment box. Frequently, this box is already open, in which case you can simply . . .

2. **Click in the text box that appears.**

3. **Type what you want to say.**

4. **When you're finished, press Enter.**

 Frequently, comment *threads,* or a series of comments, can become like an ongoing conversation. If you are responding to someone who commented above you, type the @ symbol (Shift+2) and start typing the name of the person you want to respond to. You'll be able to select their name from an auto-complete list that appears as you type.

After you comment on something, you'll be notified about subsequent comments so that you can keep up on the conversation. If you decide, on second thought, that maybe you didn't really want to say that thing, you can always delete your comment by hovering your mouse on it and clicking the X that appears. You can do the same when someone comments on something you've posted and you don't like what they have to say.

To Like something, simply click the word *Like* (it's a small blue link) below or next to the item. Your friend will be notified that you Like it. If you didn't mean it, really, click Unlike and your Like will be taken away.

Part V

Privacy and Safety on Facebook

. . . .

In This Part

▶ Navigating the Facebook privacy options

▶ Protecting yourself online and on Facebook

▶ Deciding what to share and when

. . . .

*U*nfortunately, you hear a lot of horror stories about the Internet, especially about social networking sites. Many of them involve teenagers and predators, some of them involve identity theft, and others involve far less salacious (but no less real) problems, such as spamming and computer viruses. The bad news is that these things are out there. The good news is that Facebook has some of the most granular privacy controls on the Internet, enabling you to share real information comfortably on Facebook.

Facebook has created a trusted environment that provides some major assets:

✔ **In general, people create real accounts for themselves, and people are who they say they are on Facebook.** This means that the community enforces a standard of reality. When people ask you to view their webcasts or click some mysterious link, those actions are reported by the community, and the offenders are removed from Facebook. This also means that it's usually easy to tell a real person from a fake one, and you can make informed choices about whom you interact with online.

✔ **In general, people on Facebook interact with the same people they interact with in real life.**

✔ **Facebook provides granular privacy controls that are built in to every piece of information you create on the site.**

✔ **Facebook makes it easy for you to see your own timeline as other specific people see it.** This means you can easily verify that you're sharing the information you want to share with the right set of people.

Privacy on the Go

As I mentioned, there are lots of different privacy controls on Facebook, but the one you will likely use most frequently isn't found on the Privacy Pages. It's found on your Timeline and on your home page, inside the Post box or publisher. This is the box you use to update your status, share a link, or post photos and more. Whenever you share anything from one of these boxes, next to the word "Post" is the privacy setting for that post. If you want to change the privacy settings when you're about to post something, click the current setting to expand the privacy menu. The typical privacy options are

✔ **Public or Everyone:** This means that anyone who finds your Timeline, potentially anywhere on the Internet, can see this post. This is a good setting for the things that are not very personal, or that you want to broadcast more widely.

✔ **Friends:** This means that only your friends can see that post. This is where I keep most of my posts.

✔ **Friends Except Acquaintances:** This option refers to the acquaintances smart list that Facebook creates for many users. People who have been added to this list are unable to see that post.

✔ **Only Me:** This option allows you to keep something on your profile for your own reference, but not show it to anyone else on Facebook. I don't use this setting very often for posts; when I do it's something I often change a post to after I've already posted it, when I don't want to lose the comments that have already been made.

✔ **Custom:** You can use custom settings to show posts to specific groups of people. You can choose a setting like Friends of Friends if you want something to be visible to more than just friends, but not to the public; or you can even choose to show something only to specific friends, or to hide it from specific friends.

✔ **Lists:** In addition to the custom option, you can quickly decide just to post something to a certain list of friends (one of the lists created by you, or by Facebook). This ensures that only people on that list are able to see the post.

The Privacy Pages

Anytime you want to change or check your general privacy settings, you need to go to the Privacy pages. These can be found by clicking the Account menu, the white downward-facing arrow, in the big blue bar on top, and then clicking Privacy Settings. This brings you to the Privacy page.

Control Privacy When You Post

This section is a reminder of the Privacy on the Go information. You can actually set privacy anytime you share anything using the Share menu on your timeline.

Control Your Default Privacy

Default Privacy applies to the things you post when you aren't using the Share menu. For the most part, this applies to posting via Facebook's app for mobile phones.

How You Connect

The How You Connect section is where you control the ways people can find you and interact with you on Facebook. For the most part, these settings have to do with what people can see and do on your timeline before you are friends. Click Edit Settings on the right of the How You Connect to open the How You Connect settings box, shown in Figure 5-1.

Figure 5-1: Edit how you connect to others here.

There are five settings in this section, each phrased in the form of a question. Click the drop-down menu to the right of each setting to change it. Click the Done button to close the box.

✔ **Who can look up your timeline by name or contact info?** In other words, this setting controls who can find you in search. Often people who are shy and like the sense of feeling hidden set this to Friends, but we recommend leaving it open to Everyone. This allows your friends to actually find you and become your Facebook friends.

✔ **Who can send you friend requests?** This setting determines who can request your friendship through the site. The default setting here is Everyone. This makes sense for most people because especially as you're getting started, many people you know may come across your timeline and send you a request.

 People you subscribe to can send you a friend request regardless of your friend request settings.

✔ **Who can send you Facebook Messages?** This setting determines who can send you a message through Facebook. We like leaving this set to Everyone because you never know what sort of opportunities or long-lost friends might show up and send you a message. Messages from non-friends are kept separate in your Inbox, so you don't have to worry about non-friends taking up too much space. Remember, friends can always send you messages on Facebook.

Timeline and Tagging

These settings control the ways you interact with people on your Timeline and while posting. The settings here include

✔ **Who can post on your timeline:** If you don't want your friends leaving these sorts of public messages for you (a common need if you're using Facebook as a professional or for networking), you can set this to Only Me. Remember, people who are not your friends can never post on your Timeline.

✔ **Who can see posts by others on your timeline:** Another way to control the aforementioned "embarrassing friend on your timeline" problem is to limit who can see the timeline posts your friends have left. This option opens the Audience Selector.

✔ **Review posts in which you're tagged:** This setting lets you review tags that other people post about you before they appear on your own Timeline. For example, let's say your friend Leah tagged you at a coffee shop check-in while you were supposed to be at work. If this setting were turned on, that check-in would not link back to or appear on your own timeline unless you approve it. Boss disaster averted.

✔ **Who can see posts you've been tagged in:** You can control who can see posts you've been tagged in (in other words, not a post you made, but a post that a friend made and tagged you in) when they visit your profile.

✔ **Review tags added to your posts:** Frequently on Facebook, people post a photo that has lots of people in it, and may not take the time to add tags to every face. If your friends choose to add tags, you can either let them do so, or make sure that you approve the tags before they are added.

✔ **Who sees tag suggestions for you:** One of Facebook's photo features is something called Tag Suggestions. Using Facial Recognition, Facebook might suggest adding a tag of you to a

friend when he or she adds an album to
Facebook. If you'd rather Facebook not suggest
these tags to your friends, change this setting to
No One.

Ads, Apps, and Websites

An *application* (or *app*) is a blanket term used to
describe pieces of software that use Facebook data,
even when Facebook didn't build those applications.
Developers all over the world build games, websites,
and useful tools around the data you already share on
Facebook. To make it easier to get people using these
applications, they import the data from Facebook.
When you click Edit Settings next to Ads, Apps, and
Websites, you are taken to a new page that lets you
control which applications get what data:

✔ **Apps You Use:** Lists of the applications you use,
   in order of what you've used most recently.
   Apps you use require direct permission from
   you to begin accessing your data and posting
   to your timeline.

✔ **How People Bring Your Info to the Apps They
   Use:** Even if you don't use applications, your
   friends may. You can restrict what information
   applications can see using the check boxes
   pictured in Figure 5-2.

✔ **Instant Personalization:** Instant personalization
   is a Facebook feature that lets certain Facebook
   partners access your public Facebook information using browser information, as opposed to
   using the permission dialog boxes that most
   apps use before they get access to any information. You can turn off Instant Personalization by
   clicking Edit Settings and disabling it on the
   Instant Personalization privacy page.

✔ **Public Search:** Public Search enables people who are searching your name in a search engine like Google or Bing to find your Facebook timeline in the results. You can prevent this from happening by clicking Edit Settings and disabling it on the ensuing page.

✔ **Ads:** Facebook is free for you to use, which means that the way it stays in business is chiefly by showing you ads. Because of the way people share and interact on Facebook, the company is often experimenting with ways to make ads more personalized, relevant, and social. Clicking the Edit Settings link takes you to a page that provides more information on the different features of Facebook advertising and provides you with a few options related to Ads. Please remember that you cannot simply opt to stop receiving ads; they are pretty much part of the Facebook package.

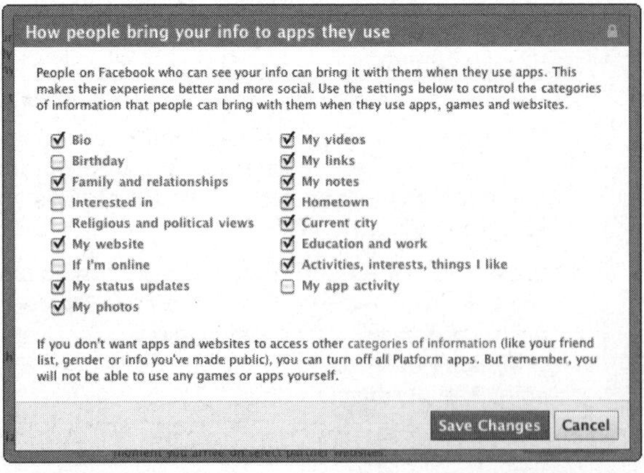

Figure 5-2: What can your friends share with apps and games?

Limit the audience for past posts

Your posts are archived on your Timeline along with
the privacy setting you made when you created them.
Were you ranting about politics publicly and now
don't want to be so partisan? You can use this setting
to go back and change all of your public posts to ones
that only friends can see. Keep in mind that this setting applies to all public posts, even non-partisan
ones.

Blocked People and Apps

Most of your privacy settings are preventative mea-
sures for making yourself comfortable on Facebook.
Block lists are usually more reactive. If someone does
something on Facebook that bothers you, you may
choose to block him.

To get to your block lists, click Manage Blocking to
the right of the Blocked People and Apps section.
This takes you to the Manage Blocking privacy page.

Block Users

Blocking someone on Facebook is the strongest way
to distance yourself from that person on Facebook.
For the most part, if you add someone to your Block
list, he can't see any traces of you on Facebook. You
won't show up in his News Feed; if he looks at a photo
in which you're tagged, he may see you in the photo
(that's unavoidable), but he won't see that your name
has been tagged. When you write on other people's
timelines, your posts are hidden from him. A few key
things to remember about blocking:

  ✔ It's almost entirely reciprocal. If you block
     someone, he is just as invisible to you as you
     are to him. So you can't access his timeline, nor
     can you see anything about him anywhere on
     the site. The only difference is that if you

blocked the relationship, you're the only one who can unblock it.

✔ People who you block are not notified that you blocked them. Nor are they notified if you unblock them. If they are perceptive Facebook users, they may notice your suspicious absence, but Facebook never tells them that you have blocked them.

✔ From someone's timeline, click the gear button at the top of his About section to open a drop-down menu with the Report/Block option. When you block someone who is a friend, you are prompted to unfriend them in addition to reporting or blocking them. If you block from the privacy page, you can enter the name or e-mail address of anyone, and you automatically unfriend (if you were friends) and block that person.

To add people to your Block list, simply enter their name or e-mail addresses into the boxes provided. Then click the Block button. Their names then appear in a list here. Click the Unblock link next to their names if you wish to remove the block.

Blocking on Facebook doesn't necessarily extend to Apps and Games you use on Facebook and around the Internet. Contact the Developers of the apps you use to learn how to block people within games and apps.

To add people to your block list, simply enter their name or e-mail address into the boxes provided. Then click the Block button. Their name appears in a list here. Click the Unblock link next to their names if you wish to remove the block.

Block App Invites

As you get going on the site, you may find out you know people who LOVE to send a ton of application invites — "Play this game! And this game! Try this! Check out this!" You might even become that person. But say that you aren't a big fan of using applications. Rather than block the overly friendly person who's sending you all those invitations, you can simply block invitations in a way that still lets you interact with your friend in every other way, but you won't receive application invites.

Block Event Invites

Similar to App Invites, you may have friends who are big planners and love to invite all of their friends to their events. These may be events that you have no chance of attending because they are taking place across the country, and your friend has chosen to invite all of his friends without any regard for location. Again, your friend is cool, but his endless unnecessary invitations are not. Instead of getting rid of your friend, you can get rid of the invitations by entering his or her name here.

What's a network?

People who join with school- or job-specific e-mails still have the opportunity to use their networks to control their privacy. Therefore, if you are a student and joined Facebook with your .edu e-mail address, you may notice that you have a few additional privacy options that include the word *Networks,* such as the ability to share a piece of content with all the members of a network, regardless of friendship status.

Custom-made privacy

If you have very specific needs, customized privacy settings may help you feel more comfortable sharing on Facebook. The Custom privacy option allows you to choose specific people (or lists of people) who can see something, or choose specific people (or lists of people) who can't see something.

Timeline Privacy

Lots of information lives on the About section at the top of your timeline. This is information that's different from the dynamic content that lives on your timeline. This information, such as where you went to school or your relationship status, changes infrequently, if ever. You can edit the privacy for this content in the same place you edit the information itself. To get there, go to your timeline and then click the Update Info button at the top of the About section.

The About page has several boxes, each representing a different information category. You can augment your Work and Education information by typing the name of your employer or school in the available text boxes. Click the Edit button in the upper-right corner of a box to access additional editing options for that category. Next to each piece of information, an icon appears signifying who can see that piece of information. By default, most of this information is set to Public and visible to Everyone, although contact information is visible only to Friends by default.

Figure 5-3 shows editing the privacy for a piece of information — in this case, the current city. Clicking the privacy icon to the right of the field displays the Audience Selector. When you've finished changing your settings for any particular category, remember to click Save wherever it appears.

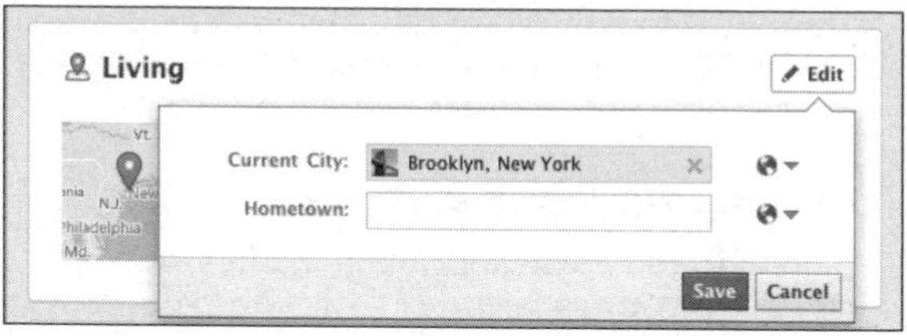

Figure 5-3: Edit privacy for every piece of information on your timeline.

Timeline information is one of the places where the Only Me setting might come in handy. For example, many people don't like sharing their birthdays on Facebook, but Facebook requires you to enter a birthday when you sign up. By making it visible only to you, it effectively hides your birthday from everyone.

> Click Save Changes when you finish editing privacy settings. Otherwise, the new settings won't stick.

Previewing Privacy

The View As setting allows you to explore how your timeline looks to other people and appears to you when you are looking at your own timeline. Click the gear button in the About section of your timeline to open a drop-down menu containing View As. Choosing this option takes you to a preview of your timeline as most people on Facebook see it. In other words, it shows you all the parts of your timeline set to Public.

You can also preview how your timeline looks to specific people by entering a name into the text field within the light blue box on top of the preview. For example, if you've purposely hidden some content from specific people, you can enter those people's

names just to double-check that you did it correctly
and that they see only what you want them to see.

Album and video privacy

Each time you create an album or add a video to
Facebook, you can use the Privacy drop-down menu
to select who can see it. These options are as follows:

- ✔ **Public or Everyone:** This setting means that
  anyone can see the album. It doesn't necessarily
  mean that everyone *will* see the album, though.
  Facebook doesn't generally display your content
  to people who are not your friend. But, if someone you didn't know searched for you and went
  to your Profile, they could see that album.

- ✔ **Only Friends:** Only confirmed friends can see the
  photos or videos when you have this setting.

- ✔ **Custom:** Custom privacy settings can be as
  closed or as open as you want. You may decide
  that you want to share an album only with the
  people who were at a particular Event, which
  you can do with a custom setting.

By default, when you start using Facebook, albums
and videos you add are visible to everyone. If you
aren't comfortable with this, remember to adjust your
privacy settings accordingly when you add new
photos and video.

Privacy settings for photos and videos of yourself

The beauty of creating albums on Facebook is that it
builds a giant cross-listed spreadsheet of information
about your photos — who is in what photos, where
those photos were taken, and so on. You're cross-
listed in photos that you own and in photos that you

don't own. However, you may want more control over these tags and who can see them. To control this, go to the Privacy Settings page from the Account menu and click Edit Settings next to the How Tags Work section. This expands a pop-up window. The settings to pay attention to in the context of photos and videos are Profile Review and Profile Visibility.

Turning on Profile Review allows you to review all the tags people add of you before those photos, videos, and other posts are actually added to your Profile. You can reject tags for photos you don't like or don't want to be associated with. Remember, just because you reject a tag doesn't mean the photo won't be added to Facebook; it just means you won't be officially marked as in it. If you really don't want a specific photo or video on Facebook, contact the friend who uploaded the content and ask them to take it down.

Profile Visibility controls who can see the content you're tagged in after you've approved the tags. In other words, just because you've approved a tag, it doesn't mean you want random people able to see those photos and videos. We keep our Profile Visibility for tags set to Friends of Friends, but if you're shyer, Friends is a good setting for this.

Taking Personal Responsibility for Safety

No one wants anything bad to happen to you because of something you do on Facebook. Facebook doesn't want that. You don't want that. We definitely don't want that. We hope that these explanations help to prevent anything bad from happening to you on Facebook. But no matter what, *you* need to take part in keeping yourself safe. In order to ensure your own safety on Facebook, you have to make an effort to be smart and safe online.

So what *is* your part? Your part is to be aware of what you're putting online and on Facebook by asking yourself a few questions:

> Is what I'm putting on Facebook legal or illegal?

> Would I be embarrassed by someone in particular finding this information?

> Will the audience with whom I'm sharing this information use it in a way I trust?

You need to be the one to choose whether displaying any given piece of information on Facebook is risky. If it's risky, you need to be the one to figure out the correct privacy settings for showing this information to the people you choose to see it — and not to the people you don't.

Remembering That It Takes a Village

Another way in which you (and every member of Facebook) contribute to keeping Facebook a safe, clean place is in the reports that you submit about spam, harassment, inappropriate content, and fake timelines. Facebook assumes that your friends aren't putting up bad stuff, but when you're looking at content of people you're not directly connected to, you should see a little Report link beneath it. This is true for Photos, Timelines, Groups, Links, Applications, Pages — and more. When you click one of these links, you see the Report page. Figure 5-4 shows an example of someone reporting an inappropriate photo. (Photo not pictured, for obvious reasons — sorry.)

Figure 5-4: Reporting inappropriate content.

Sometimes something that you report may be offensive to you but doesn't violate the Statement of Rights and Responsibilities and, therefore, will remain on Facebook. Due to privacy restrictions, User Operations may not always notify you about actions taken as a result of your support, but rest assured that the team handles every report.

Peeking Behind the Scenes

Facebook's part in keeping everyone safe requires a lot of manpower and technology power. The labor involves responding to the reports that you and the rest of Facebook submit, as well as proactively going into Facebook and getting rid of content that violates the Statement of Rights and Responsibilities. But, so you know that Facebook is actively thinking about user safety and privacy, we talk about a few of the general areas where Facebook does a lot of preventive work.

✔ **Protecting minors:** People under the age of 18 have special visibility and privacy rules applied to them. For example, users under the age of 18 don't have Public Search Listings created for them. Other proprietary systems are in place that are alerted if a person is interacting with the timelines of minors in ways they shouldn't, as well as systems that get alerted when someone targets an ad to minors.

✔ **Preventing spam and viruses:** The spam reports that you provide are incredibly helpful. Facebook also has a bunch of systems that keep track of the sort of behavior that spammers tend to do.

✔ **Preventing phishing:** *Phishing* is a term that refers to malicious websites attempting to gain sensitive information (like usernames and passwords to online accounts) by masquerading as the sites you use and trust. Just like spam and virus prevention, Facebook has a series of proprietary systems in place to try to break this cycle. If you do have the misfortune to get phished (and it can happen to the best of us), you may run into one of the systems that Facebook uses to help people take back their timelines and protect themselves from phishing in the future. Similarly, remember that Facebook will never ask you to e-mail them your password. If you receive an e-mail asking for something like that, report it as spam immediately.

If you want to stay up-to-date with the latest scams on Facebook, or want more information about protecting yourself, you can Like Facebook's Security Page at www.facebook. com/security. This provides you with ongoing information about safety and security on Facebook.

Part VI

Facebook Applications

- -

In This Part

▶ Uploading photos and videos

▶ Editing and tagging photos, videos, and notes

▶ Writing notes

- -

Many Facebook users share the sensation of getting "lost" in Facebook — not in a bad way, but like you lose yourself in a good book. Often, this happens with News Feed or a friend's timeline. You click an appealing photo, which leads you to an album you like, which leads you to a video from a friend's vacation, which leads you to another friend who has a ton of new notes about her life. And the next thing you know, your editor is tapping you on the shoulder and saying, "Did you finish writing that chapter about photos yet?"

Managing Photos

Facebook Photos is the leading photo-sharing application on the web. This may sound surprising because entire sites are dedicated to storing, displaying, and sharing photos, whereas, Photos is just one piece of the Facebook puzzle. However, the fact that all of your friends are likely on Facebook and using Photos makes it a one-stop shop for tracking all the photos of you, all the photos you've taken, and all the photos of your friends.

Facebook is a great place to keep your photos and videos because you can easily organize them into albums and share them with all the people who may want to see them. You can upload these items for Events such as parties and trips, for a collection of photos to show people, or for a silly video of you and your friends that you took with a cell phone.

From the Publisher, you can click the Photo/Video link to post photos. When you do so, you see something like Figure 6-1. This screen gives you options for how you want to upload your content.

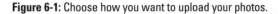

Figure 6-1: Choose how you want to upload your photos.

The Photo Publisher options include the following, and I'll go through each one at a time:

✔ **Upload a Photo or Video:** Use this option if you have one funny photo you want to share by posting it to your Wall. When you upload a single photo, it is added to an album that Facebook creates called Wall Photos.

✔ **Use Webcam:** If you have a webcam built into or attached to your computer, you can take a photo and post it directly to your Wall. When you add a

webcam photo, it is added to an album created
by Facebook called Webcam Photos.

✔ **Create an Album:** Use this option when you
want to really show off a series of photos.
Choosing this option starts the process detailed
in the upcoming section, "Creating an album."

Uploading a single photo or video

Say you have just one great photo you want to share.
To get started, follow these steps:

1. **Click Add Photo in the Publisher on your Home
   page or Timeline.**

2. **Click Upload a Photo or Video.**

3. **Click Choose File or Browse (the exact wording
   may depend on your browser and operating
   system).**

   This opens a window that allows you to browse
   your computer's hard drive and select the photo
   or video you want.

4. **Click the photo or video you want to share to
   select it.**

5. **Click Open or Choose (the wording may depend
   on your browser and operating system).**

   This brings you back to Facebook. There should
   be a filename of some sort next to the Choose File
   button.

6. **Click in the Say Something box and type any
   explanation you think is necessary.**

7. **(Optional) Click the Privacy menu to select who
   can see this photo or video.**

   If you've never changed your privacy settings, by
   default, everyone on Facebook can see your content if they navigate to your Timeline.

8. **Click Post.**

   This officially posts the photo or video to
   Facebook and creates a post that people can see
   in your Timeline and in their News Feeds (if they
   are allowed by your privacy settings to see the
   photo). By default, photos are added to an album
   called Timeline Photos, which is a collection of
   all the photos you've ever added individually.
   Videos are added to an album called Videos.

Recording video or taking a picture

If you have a webcam either built into or attached to
your computer, you can record videos straight to
Facebook and take photos that are instantly posted.

1. **Choose Add Photo/Video in the Publisher.**

2. **Click Use Webcam.**

   This expands the Publisher and turns on your
   webcam. By default, it will be in Video mode, so
   click the photo icon in the upper-right corner to
   switch to video. You should see yourself (or
   wherever your webcam is pointed) within the
   Publisher. Note that you aren't yet recording.

3. **Click the red button in the middle of the screen
   to start recording or to take a photo.**

   Skip Step 4 if you're taking photos, not video.

4. **Click the button again to stop recording.**

5. **Press Play to watch the clip and make sure
   you're happy with it.**

   Or, look at the photo and make sure you're happy
   with it. If you don't like it, click Reset and start
   over.

6. **(Optional) Type any explanation or comment into the Say Something About This Video box.**

7. **(Optional) Select who can see this video using the Privacy drop-down menu.**

   As usual, your basic options are Everyone, Friends of Friends, Only Friends, or a Customized group of people.

8. **Click Post.**

   The video is posted to your Timeline and may appear in your friends' News Feeds.

Adding an album

Adding an entire photo album isn't that different from adding a single photo. It all starts from the publisher:

1. **Click Add Photo/Video in the publisher.**

2. **Click Create Photo Album.**

   This opens a window that allows you to browse your computer's hard drive and select the photos you want. You can select up to 200 photos for one album.

3. **Click Choose or Open.**

   The photo upload begins immediately. You see a progress bar on the Facebook screen. After the photos are uploaded, they appear in order onscreen as well.

4. **(Optional) Add comments, tags, or other edits to your album.**

   I discuss this in the next section.

5. **(Optional) Select who can see this album using the Privacy drop-down menu at the bottom of the page.**

6. Click the Post Photos button.

   The album is posted to your Timeline and may appear in your friends' News Feeds.

After uploading the photos for your album, you have several editing options. You can move photos around, add captions and additional tags, as well as change any info you entered when you set up the album, like name or location. You can also add or remove photos from the album you have created. All of these actions can be done fairly easily from the album view.

Editing and tagging photos

After uploading photos to your album, you have several editing options:

> ✔ **Edit Album Name, Location, Description, and Privacy:** Above the top row of photos are spaces to enter this information.
>
>   If you've already posted the album, you can edit this information by navigating to the Photos section of your Timeline, clicking on the Album you want to edit, and then clicking Edit on the album you'd like to change. The Edit Album page is shown in Figure 6-2.

Figure 6-2: Edit your Album here.

Click Done when you finish making edits to the album.

✔ **Delete an album:** While you're looking at the Edit Album page, look for a trash can icon at the top of the page. If you ever decide, in retrospect, that adding a particular album was a poor choice, you can click Delete Album to remove the whole thing.

 If you delete your photo album, all the photos in it will be gone forever, along with any comments people have made on it. So make sure you want to get rid of it completely before you delete it.

✔ **Reorder photos in the album:** Chances are that if you added your photos in bulk, they don't appear exactly in the right order. And it's awkward when the photos of the sunset appear first, and the photos of your awesome day of adventure come afterward. To reorder photos from the Edit Album page, drag and drop them into the order you want.

✔ **Add more photos:** After you've created a photo album, you can add more photos to it at any time. Sometimes, depending on how organized the photos on your hard drive are, you may want to add photos in batches anyhow.

✔ **Add a tag to an individual photo:** If you skipped adding tags earlier, you can always add your tags to individual photos.

✔ **Rotate a photo:** Many times, photos wind up being sideways. It's a result of turning your camera to take a vertical shot as opposed to a horizontal one.

✔ **Add a description to an individual photo:** Just as you can add a description to the album as a whole, you can add descriptions or captions to individual photos.

✔ **Delete a photo from an album:** Maybe you realized that not all 20 group shots from the high school reunion have to go in the album, or that one photo has a whole bunch of crossed eyes. You can remove photos entirely from an album.

 To edit an album at any time, click Photos in the left column on your Home page and then select My Uploads. Click Edit Album beneath the album title you want to modify.

Editing and tagging videos

When we talk about editing videos that you've added, we don't mean the kind of fancy editing that editing software like Final Cut Pro might do. Rather, you're editing how these items are displayed and seen by your friends. To get to the Edit Video screen, begin to play the video. To the right of the video is where comments and Likes appear. Click Edit to open a few fields that can be changed at any time, as shown in Figure 6-3.

Figure 6-3: Edit your video's info here.

The Edit Video screen has several fields to fill out; most of these are optional:

- ✔ **Description:** This field is for you to describe what's happening in your video, although frequently videos speak for themselves.

- ✔ **Who were you with?:** This option is similar to tagging a photo or a note. Simply start typing the names of all the friends who are in the video and then select the correct friends from the list that appears. Your friends are notified that they've been tagged in a video and can remove the tag if they decide they don't want to be forever remembered as *the one who got pied in the face*.

- ✔ **Where were you?** Adding a location to a video helps answer the most common question you'll get in the comments: "Where were you when this happened??"

- ✔ **Date:** You can also add a date, usually of when the video was taken, so it can be added to the right spot on your Timeline.

- ✔ **Privacy:** Your privacy options for videos are on a per-video basis. Thus, you can choose that everyone sees *Pie in the Face,* but only certain friends (with strong stomachs) see *Pie-eating Contest.*

Click Done Editing when you finish filling out these fields.

Taking Notes

Notes are blogs. Like blogs, Notes are ways of writing entries about your life, your thoughts, or your all-time favorite songs and then sharing them with your Facebook friends. The beauty of Notes lies in the ability to blog without needing to distribute a web address to friends so that they can go check out your blog. Instead, your friends are connected to your Profile. Therefore, when you publish a Note, it appears in their News Feeds.

Writing a note

No specific rules of etiquette dictate the proper length of notes or even the contents of notes. Some people like to keep them short and informative; other people like to take the extra space to say everything they want to say about a topic. Go crazy, or not. Feeling uninspired? Pick a favorite funny memory, awkward moment, or topic that really gets people thinking. A very common note that people write on Facebook is titled "25 Things About Me," where they detail 25 facts about their lives. Getting started on your first note is pretty straightforward:

1. **From your home page, look on the left side of the page for Notes. It's in the Apps menu.**

   This takes you to Notes.

2. **Click the Write a Note button at the upper right of the page.**

   A blank note appears, as shown in Figure 6-4.

3. **In the Title field, type the title of your Note.**

4. **In the Body field, start writing about whatever interests you.**

   Facebook offers basic formatting options through the little buttons on top of the Body field. You probably recognize these from your word processing programming. The B icon makes text **bold,** the I icon makes text *italicized,* and so on. You can also create numbered or bulleted lists, as well as block quotes. The Preview function within Notes is a good way to figure out whether your formatting is working the way you want it to. To find out quickly whether your HTML tags are working, you can toggle between the Preview and Edit screens.

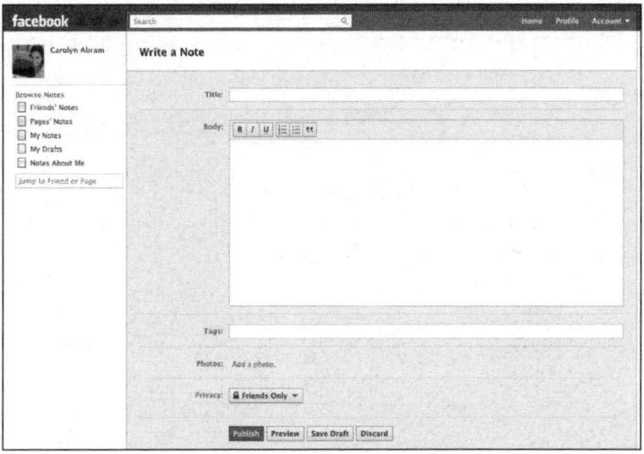

Figure 6-4: The startling white canvas of a blank note staring at you.

5. **Tag friends who appear in your note by typing their names into the Tags field.**

   Facebook attempts to auto-complete as you type. When you see the name you're looking for appear, highlight it and click Enter to select it.

6. **Click the Add a Photo link to add photos.**

7. **Choose who can see your note using the Privacy drop-down menu.**

8. **After you finish writing, click Preview to view what your note will look like when published. Or click Save Draft if you want to come back to the Note later.**

Preview opens a preview of the Note, so you can have one last glance-over before you publish it. If you're unhappy with your preview, click the Edit button to return to the Create Note screen.

You can come back to your draft at any time by clicking the My Drafts menu item. You'll see this on the left column of the page when you come to the Notes tab of your Profile.

9. **When you're happy with your Note, click Publish.**

Congrats! You shared your Note and your thoughts with your friends. They can now read, like, and comment on your Notes.

Part VII

Getting Organized with Groups and Events

- -

In This Part

▶ Learning about and finding Groups

▶ Creating and administering Groups

▶ Learning about and finding Events

▶ Creating and administering your own Events

- -

*G*roups of people exist for all of us in real life. Facebook gives us a way to represent and organize these groups. Groups on Facebook are designed to help you communicate with real-world groups of people, whether that's a big group like Ottawa University's Class of 1958 reunion or a small group like Beach Trip Next Weekend. Like everything on Facebook, you decide who can participate and what they can see.

And after you've formed your Group connection on Facebook, you can use Events to plan a get together. Not much of a party planner? No worries. Facebook also handles the planning of smaller, more impromptu Events. You can easily collect a crew for dinner or for Frisbee in the park.

Getting Going with Groups

Groups function in large part like a Profile owned by all the people who are part of the Group. To get started with Groups, create one. As your Friend List grows, and as you get involved in more and more activities on and off Facebook, it's inevitable that at some point you will want to create a Group to make sharing with certain people easier. For example, if you like to talk with certain people about certain types of news or if you want to share photos just with family, you can create a Group to facilitate these activities.

Anatomy of a Group

The first thing you see when you visit a Group is its Home page, as shown in Figure 7-1. To get to a Group Home page, just click the Group name in the left side column. If you have a lot of Groups, you may need to click a More link to find the one you want to get to. Just as your Profile provides a summary of you (not to say that *you* could ever be summarized), this page provides an overview of what's happened in the Group recently, including snapshots of the most recent photos, videos, and member comments.

At the top part of the Group Home page, you see the Group name (in this case, Dummy Group) and the Group privacy level (in this case, Closed). Depending on privacy settings, you may be able to see all of a Group's contents before joining it, even though you can't post new content.

Moving down the central column of the page, you'll see something fairly recognizable: the Wall. People can post content, events, and ideas to the Wall, where other members of the Group can respond via comments. And of course, at the very top of the Wall is a Publisher,

where you can write posts, add photos or videos, ask
Questions, and create Files (which are wiki-style docu-
ments that all Group members can edit).

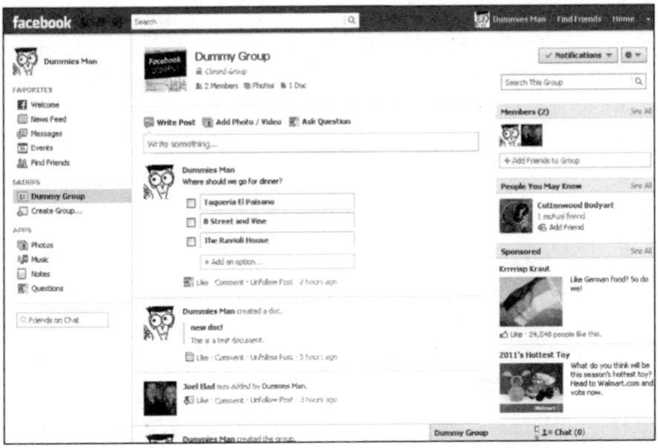

Figure 7-1: Welcome to the Dummy Group.

On the right side of the page are a few buttons, links,
and boxes. Starting at the top and moving down the
page:

✔ **Notifications button:** Click this button in the
  top-right corner of the page to manage notifications that you receive from this Group and to
  edit your settings for the group.

✔ **Gear button:** Click the drop-down arrow next to
  the Gear button to bring up most of your
  options for this group, including the following:

  • *Chat with Group:* Click this link to initiate a
    Group Chat — in other words, to talk in real-
    time with all the members of the Group who
    happen to be online. This option is only avail-
    able if the person who first created the group,
    or one of the admins, chooses to enable it.

- *Create Event:* Click this link to create a new Event for the Group.

- *Edit Group (admins only):* If you are a Group admin, you can click this button to access certain Group settings that only you control. This is talked about more in the upcoming "Being a Group administrator" section.

- *Report Group:* If you feel that this group is violating one of Facebook's policies in some way, you can pick this option to alert Facebook so it can decide whether to close this group.

- *Leave Group:* Turns out the No Boys Allowed Club is somewhat dull? Letting your membership in the Community Theater lapse for a season? If at any time you want out, all you have to do is click this link.

If you remove yourself from a Group, you cannot rejoin, and your friends cannot invite you to rejoin.

✔ **Search This Group:** This text box at the top-right corner of the page allows you to search the content of a Group for specific keywords. It only searches text that Group members have entered, so if you're searching for a particular link someone shared, you'll have to find the person who sent it.

Search results within Groups show the context and the keyword, as well as an icon to represent that the word was found in a comment (quotation mark icons) or an original post (sticky note icon).

✔ **Members:** At the top of the right column is a samll gray link that displays the number of members in the group. Click this link to view a list of all members.

✔ **Add Friends to Group box:** If someone adds you to a Group and you know other people who ought to be there, click inside this text box to type in their names and add whomever you want.

Creating your own Groups

As a Group's creator, you're by default the *Group administrator,* which means that you write the Group's information, control its privacy settings, and generally keep it running smoothly. You can also promote other members of the Group to administrators to grant them the same privileges and then they can help you with these responsibilities.

Here are the steps you follow to create a Group:

1. **Click Create Group from the left side menu.**

   The Create Group box appears (see Figure 7-2).

Create New Group

Group Name:

Members:

Privacy: ○ 🌐 **Open**
Anyone can see the group, who's in it, and what members post.

⦿ 🔒 **Closed**
Anyone can see the group and who's in it. Only members see posts.

○ ⊘ **Secret**
Only members see the group, who's in it, and what members post.

Learn more about groups privacy

Create   Cancel

Figure 7-2: The Create New Group box.

2. **Enter a Group name into the Group Name field.**

   Choose something descriptive, if possible, so when you add people to it, they'll know what they are getting into.

3. **Add members by typing their names into the Members field.**

   At this time, you can add only friends as members. Facebook tries to auto-complete your friends' names as you type. When you see the name you want, press Enter to select it. You can add as many — or as few — friends as you like. If you forget someone, you can always add him or her later.

4. **Choose the privacy level for your Group.**

   There are three privacy options for Groups:

   • *Open:* Open Groups are entirely available to the public. Anyone can join simply by clicking a join button; anyone can see all the content the Group posts. This type of Group is best for a very public organization that wants to make it easy for people to join and contribute.

   • *Closed:* By default, your Group is set to Closed. This means that anyone can see the list of members, but only members can see the content posted to the Group by its members. People can request to join the Group, but admins (like you) need to approve that request before they can see Group info.

   • *Secret:* Secret Groups are virtually invisible on the site to people who haven't been added to the Group. No one but members can see the member list and the content posted. But remember, people who have been added to the Group can also add their friends, so if you are protecting state secrets, you might want to find a more secure method. I recommend carrier pigeons.

5. **Click Create.**

Congrats, your Group has been created. You can now start sharing!

Sharing with your Group

The whole point of creating or joining a Group is to enable communication, so get started communicating! Ways that you can get involved include posting on the Group Wall, chatting with Group members, creating Docs and Events, and commenting on Group posts.

Posting to the Group Wall is the same as posting to your own Wall or to a friend's Wall. Clicking what you want to share (Post, Photo/Video, or Question) and then following the onscreen prompts is all you have to do to put your content out there.

The important thing to remember is that when you share something from a Group, you're sharing it only with the members of that Group.

 If you're a member of a Group, you need to remember that you might not be friends with everyone in the Group. In a big Group, you might actually be sharing with more people who couldn't typically see the things you post.

Write Post

Posts are status updates that you share only with the members of a Group (unless the Group is open, in which case anyone can see your post). You might post an update just to say hi or to start a discussion with Group members. To write a post, follow these steps:

1. **Click into the Write Something text box at the top of the Group page.**

   After you click into the box, you see the Post button appear below the text box along with buttons to indicate where you are and which other Facebook members are with you.

2. **Type whatever you want to say into the box.**

   For the Dummies Group, this might be something like "What do people think of the new Groups?" or "Does anyone know how I can start Group Chat?"

3. **Click Post.**

   Your post appears on the Group wall, and Group members see it in their notifications and possibly in their News Feeds.

Photo or Video

Sometimes, writing a post won't do for the current circumstances. For example, if I want my fellow dummies to know that I received the most recent edition of *Facebook For Dummies,* I could tell them by writing a post to the effect of "Hey, dummies, I got my copy of the new book." Or, I could *show* them by doing the following:

1. **Click Photo/Video in the Publisher (at the top of the Group page).**

   The Photo Publisher appears.

2. **Click Use Webcam (only if you have a webcam).**

3. **Pose for the camera.**

   Remember to smile.

4. **(Optional) Add a comment about the photo in the Say Something box.**

5. **Click Post.**

   The post appears on the Group Wall, and all members (depending on notification settings) are notified about your post. They can then comment and be part of what you are sharing.

Similar to photos, sometimes videos are simply meant to be shared. Maybe you have a video from your most recent Ultimate Frisbee game or from a family trip. This is a great way to share it just with family members and to be certain they are able to see it. To post a video, follow these steps:

1. **Click Photo/Video in the Publisher at the top of the Group Wall.**

2. **Select either Use Webcam (only if you have a webcam) or Upload Photo/Video.**

   For this example, say you want to upload a video you recorded at another time. Clicking Upload Photo/Video expands the Publisher.

3. **Click Browse.**

   A dialog box appears that allows you to select a file from your computer.

4. **Navigate to the video you want and click Select.**

5. **(Optional) Type some thoughts into the box above the Browse button.**

You might want to explain why you thought the video would be of interest to your fellow members. Or you can say nothing and let the video speak for itself.

6. **Click Post.**

   The video then appears on the Group Wall and in members' notifications and News Feeds.

Being a Group administrator

If you are a creator of a Group, you are automatically its *admin* or administrator. Additionally, you can be added as an admin of someone else's Group. After you have members in your Group, you can use the Group member list to remove (and even permanently ban) undesirable members, promote your most trusted members to administrators, or demote your existing administrators (if any) back to regular members.

To get you started in your career as an admin, take a look at the Edit Group page. You get to this page by clicking the Edit Group link from the drop-down list you get by clicking the Gear button at the top right of the Group Home page. Does it look a little familiar? It should look a little like your Edit Profile page, albeit with fewer sections.

First, you can add a Profile picture that appears as a thumbnail next to your Group's name. To add a thumbnail, click either the Browse or the Take a Picture button. If you select Browse, navigate to your computer's folders to find your desired photo. After you select the photo, click Open or Save or Select.

After you select the image or use your webcam to take a picture, the picture appears on the screen.

You can scroll down to update the Basic Information for the Group. If you're the creator of the Group, this page should look familiar to you. It has many of the same options you had when you created this Group:

 Click Save when you're done editing your Group's information; otherwise, all your hard work will be lost.

As an admin, you can remove and ban members from the Group, as well as create other admins to help shoulder the burden of admin-hood.

To edit members, follow these steps:

1. **Below the Group header, in the middle of the page, click the Members link.**

   This takes you to the Members page.

2. **Click the gear icon below their name and info.**

   This brings up a menu with two options: Make Admin or Remove from Group.

3. **Confirm your choice and return to your group.**

Reporting offensive Groups

If you stumble upon an offensive Group in your travels, you should report it to Facebook so that the company can take appropriate actions. To report a Group, follow these steps:

1. **Click the Gear button on the right side of the Group's Home page, and then select the Report Group link.**

2. **Fill out the report by choosing a reason for the report and include a comment that explains why you feel the Group should be removed.**

3. **Click Submit.**

Many Groups on Facebook take strong stands on controversial issues, such as abortion or gun control. In an effort to remain neutral and promote debate, Facebook won't remove a Group because you disagree with its statements.

Getting Going with Events

Events is an application built by Facebook. To access its dashboard, click Events in the left menu of your Home page. This brings you to the Events page and opens up additional menu options for Events. The Events page (shown in Figure 7-3) that you land on displays all upcoming birthdays and Facebook Events that have you on their guest lists. This includes Events you were invited to and Events you joined. You can view the events on a calendar or as a list.

To see more information about an Event, click its title to view the Event's Home page, which contains a detailed overview of the Event. Facebook also embeds a summary of the most important information — the Event's date and time, who invited you, and how many people are attending— directly into the Event listing. Wherever you find an Event listing on Facebook — say, News Feed or a Profile Wall — this information is displayed.

Figure 7-3: The Events application's Home page.

When you are through looking at upcoming Events, you can also use the submenu on the left side to navigate to your friends' Events.

Anatomy of an Event

An Event is represented on Facebook through its Home page, such as the one shown in Figure 7-4. A Home page evolves throughout the life cycle of an Event. Before the Event takes place, its Home page serves as an invitation and offers critical information for attendees, such as the Event's date and location. An Event's Home page also tracks who will or might attend the Event so that its host can plan accordingly.

Figure 7-4: An Event's Home page.

An Event's Home page is divided into two columns. The skinny column on the left is where the Event Profile picture lives, as well as information about who is and is not attending. The main column in the center of the page displays all the relevant Event information and the Event Wall.

In the main center column, here's what you can learn:

- ✔ **Event Name:** It's big and at the top of the page in black — the name your host has given to the Event.

- ✔ **Inviter (pre-RSVP):** Before you RSVP, you see the name of the person who invited you to the Event right below the Event's name. There's a difference between being invited to something by a good friend and being invited by a more

distant acquaintance, so this is good information to know before you RSVP.

✔ **Share (pre-RSVP):** The Share link scattered
throughout Facebook allows you to share
interesting content quickly with your friends,
either by sending it to them in a message, or
by posting it on your Profile, to your friend's
Wall, or to a group Wall. The Share button
allows you to share an Event along with a preview containing the Event's name, description,
and picture.

✔ **RSVP buttons (pre-RSVP):** Across from the
Event name, toward the top-right corner of the
page, you should see three big buttons: Join,
Maybe, and Decline. Click the proper button to
RSVP.

✔ **Attendance Status (post-RSVP):** If you've
already said you'll be going to an Event, the
space where the RSVP buttons were will become
a button displaying your attendance status.

If you want to change your RSVP, click your current attendance status, which opens a drop-
down menu of attendance options. Choose your
new RSVP by clicking your desired response,
and then click the RSVP button to save it.

✔ **Event Privacy:** Under the event's name, you see
a notice about whether the Event is public or
private. There's more information about Event
Privacy when you learn how to create your own
Event in the next section of this chapter.

✔ **Event Info:** This area is further divided into con-
venient sections to show you the when (Time),
where (Location), who (Created By), and what
(More Info) of the Event.

✔ **The Wall:** The Event Wall, like the Wall on your Profile, is where Event guests can leave messages, photos, videos, and relevant links for all the guests to share. In general, the Wall is where people explain why they can't make an Event, or where they express their enthusiasm about coming to an Event.

The left column, which is topped by the Event Profile Picture, contains information about invitations. Assuming you're looking at a Public Event, after you RSVPed, you'll see a button just beneath it that you can click to Select Guests to Invite. Clicking this will bring up a Friend Selector that you can use to invite your friends as well. We go over the Friend Selector later in this chapter when we go through the Event creation process.

The rest of the left column is dedicated to guests: Who is confirmed as going, who is a maybe, who hasn't replied yet, and who has declined to attend. The Attending list is on top and shows you names and thumbnails of guests. If you're not sure if you want to go to a party, this section might help you make up your mind. If you're more curious who *isn't* going, you need to click View on the Not Attending section to view that list.

Creating Your Own Events

Tired of being a *guest?* Ready to be in charge? Want to host your own Event, have complete control over the guest list, and almost single-handedly decide who among us is *in* and *out?* Let's get down to business — the business of organizing and hosting fun Events. If you're planning an Event that's not happening for a few days or so, start with the Big Events section. If your Event is more spontaneous, or perhaps has already started, skip ahead to the Quick Events section.

Big Events

Whatever actions have transpired before you log in to Facebook — a conversation about how awesome a surprise party would be, a sudden urge to give all of your friends free food in honor of the season — after you've logged in, creating an Event is easy. To begin, take the following steps:

1. **Click Events in the left column of the Home page.**

   This takes you to the Events Home page.

2. **Click the Create an Event button at the upper-right side of the page.**

   This opens the Create an Event dialog box.

3. **Fill out your Event's info:**

   You can fill out a number of fields:

   - **Name:** Enter the name of your event here, not your own name.

   - **Details:** Use this space to describe what sort of event it is, what will be happening there, the best way to park in your neighborhood, or other details you think are relevant for guests to know.

   - **Where:** Telling people where to go is generally helpful if you want people to show up. This isn't always the street address, but the name of the venue, like Mark's house or Olive Garden. Facebook tries to autocomplete the name of your venue as you type. When you

see the location's name appear, click it to
select it. If it's a Place Page, Facebook displays a link to that Page so people can find
out more.

- **When:** By default, Facebook assumes you are
an impromptu party planner, so this box
shows a party happening later today. Click
the calendar icon to change the date, and
type in the time you are hosting the event.

- **End Time (click Add End Time):** In case
you're worried about your guests overstaying
their welcome, you can include an end time in
your invitation. The link to add an end time
won't appear until you've entered a start
time.

- **Privacy:** There are three privacy options for
events: Public, Friends, and Invite Only.
Public Events can be found and attended by
anyone on Facebook. An event visible by
Friends can be seen by any of your Facebook
friends, and they are able to request an invite.
An Invite Only event is only visible to those
people that you've selected to invite.

4. **Click Invite Friends to begin to invite friends.**

Doing so brings up the Friend Selector (shown in
Figure 7-5). Simply click a friend's name or Profile
picture to select them. Click again to take them
off the list. Use the search box at the top to filter
down to a friend by name. When you are done,
click Save and Close. You can invite friends
who aren't on Facebook by adding their e-mail
addresses to the box at the bottom of the Friend
Selector.

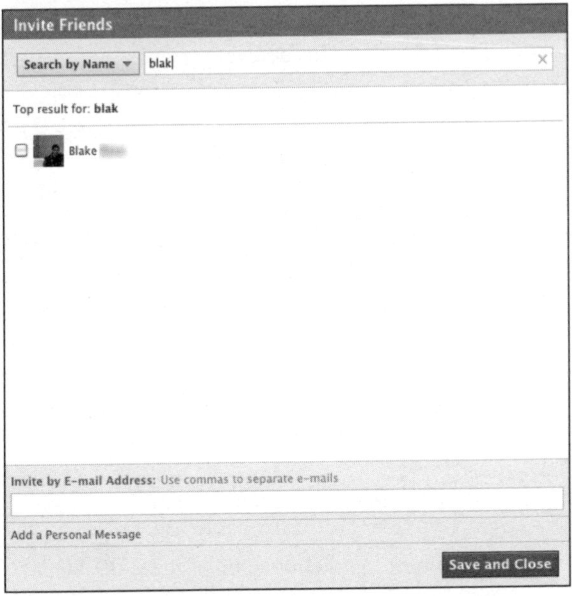

Figure 7-5: The Friend Selector helps you invite guests.

5. **(Invite Only options) Decide if you want to show the guest list or allow friends to invite their friends.**

   Keeping your guest list visible is a nice way for friends to know who else is going to an Event. This makes it easy for them to coordinate rides or plan presents, or whatever it is people do before your parties. If you don't want people to see this because of your friends' VIP status, deselect the Show the Guest List on the Event Page box. Additionally, allowing guests to invite their friends makes it easy for plus-ones to be added, but if you need to keep the guest list tight, you can prevent them from doing so without asking you to help.

6. Click Create.

This brings you to the Event page.

7. Add a photo for your Event.

Adding a photo to represent your Event makes it look pretty and inviting to your guests when they see the Event — both on the Event Home page and in invitation requests. Big, official Events often have their flier as the picture. To add an image, follow these steps:

   a. Hover over the light blue calendar place-holder. A link to Add Event Photo appears.

   b. Click Add Event Photo.

   c. Click the Browse or Choose File button to open your computer's standard interface for finding a file.

   d. Navigate to (and select) the picture on your computer that you want to use.

The picture you choose must meet the file size and type requirements outlined on the page. Currently that is a 4MB maximum. If you're not sure whether your desired picture meets the requirements, select the picture and continue with these steps. Facebook notifies you if the picture you choose can't be used.

After you've selected a photo, Facebook adds it to your Event.

Event created. Invitations sent. And you didn't have to lick a stamp. You land on your Event's Home page. Welcome home.

As soon as you click Create Event, all of your guests receive the information you just filled out. Double-check to make sure the time, date, and spelling are all correct before clicking.

Managing Your Event

You can do a number of things when you finish creating your Event and people start to join. These actions are visible and available only to you and other administrators. This section outlines the additional power you wield as an Event administrator.

Editing your Event's Info

Need to update the Event time or add info about a dress code? You can do this at any time by clicking Edit Event on the far top right of your Event page, above where the ads in the right column are. This takes you to the Edit Event page. You can edit everything about the Event. Just remember to click Save Event when you are done.

Canceling the Event

As they say, the best laid plans . . . go oft awry. If your life has gone a bit awry and ruined your Event plans, not to worry — it's easy to cancel your Event and send apologies to your guests. After clicking Edit Event in the upper right of the Event Page, you see the now familiar edit Event page, with one addition: a Cancel This Event link in the lower-right corner (sort of parallel to the Save Event button). Clicking Cancel This Event brings up a pop-up confirmation window.

Managing your Event's guest list

After guests RSVP to your Event, use the Event guest list to remove (or even permanently ban) undesirable guests, promote your most trusted guests to hosts, or demote your existing hosts (if any) to regular guests.

1. **Click the Going link under your Event photo.**

   The View Guest List box opens.

2. **Use the link to the right of each guest name that corresponds to the action you want to take.**

   For instance, to make a member an administrator, click the Make Admin button. As an administrator, the member has the same privileges — inviting people, changing Event info, messaging guests, and so on — that you do.

   You can also use the X to remove a guest from the Event. If you select this option, you can also choose to ban that person permanently so he may not rejoin the Event in the future. Banning someone is useful if the person is posting offensive content or otherwise stirring up trouble.

You can also invite more people by clicking the Select Guest to Invite button underneath the Event photo. This opens a Friend Selector, just like the one you used when creating the Event.

Part VIII

Facebook on the Go

• •

In This Part

▶ Capturing and sharing the moment with Facebook Mobile uploads

▶ Keeping yourself connected with Facebook Mobile notifications and texts

▶ Staying up-to-date with Facebook Mobile

• •

*F*acebook Mobile serves the function of making your life easier and a little more connected. Sometimes you need *something,* say, a phone number, an address, or the start time of an Event. Maybe you're sitting on a bus and want to see what your friends are up to. Maybe you just saw something ah-mazing and want all your friends to see a photo of it. Perhaps you hit it off with someone new and would like to find out whether she's romantically available before committing yourself to an awkward conversa-tion about exchanging phone numbers. (Just a heads-up: This conversation can be awkward even *if* you find that person is single. Facebook can do a lot for you, but not everything.)

In this part, I make a foolish assumption: I assume that you have a mobile phone and know how to use its features. If you don't have a phone, you may con-sider buying one after reading this chapter; this stuff is way cool. Mobile texts simply require that you own a phone and an accompanying plan that enables you to send text messages. Facebook Mobile requires a mobile data plan (that is, access to the Internet on your phone). Facebook applications require that you own any one of the several types of phones that Facebook can currently support.

Is That Facebook Mobile in Your Pocket . . . ?

In many ways, using a mobile phone can augment your experience of using Facebook on the computer. This first section is about how you can easily add information to and get information from Facebook when you're not physically in front of the computer. These features are primarily for people who do most of their Facebooking on the computer, but sometimes interact through their phone.

Getting started

To get started with Facebook Mobile, you first need to enter and confirm your phone number into the settings page:

1. **Choose Account Settings from the Account menu in the upper-right corner of the big blue bar on top.**

2. **Click the Mobile tab on the left side of the page.**

3. **Click the green Add a Phone button.**

   This opens the Activate Facebook Texts dialog box.

4. **Choose your country and your mobile carrier.**

    If your carrier isn't listed, sadly you may be out of luck for using Facebook from your mobile phone.

5. **Click Next.**

    This brings you to Step 2, which you actually have to do from your phone.

6. **From your phone, text the letter F to 32665 (FBOOK).**

    FBOOK texts you back a confirmation code. This can take a few minutes, so be patient.

7. **Enter your confirmation code into the empty box.**

8. **Choose whether you want your phone number added to your Profile via the Add This Phone Number to My Profile check box.**

    We find friends sharing their mobile numbers on Facebook useful because it allows us to use Facebook as a virtual phonebook. But if you're not comfortable with that, simply deselect the check box.

9. **Click Next.**

    This confirms your phone and brings you to set up for Facebook Texts. Your phone also receives a confirmation text with some instructions.

Mobile uploads

After a social gathering, plug your camera into a regular computer, weed out the bad photos, and upload the rest to a photo album. However, if you're the mobile photo taker, Facebook Mobile Photos is for you. With mobile photos, you have no time for weeding, editing, or second thoughts. Mobile photos pave the way to instantaneous documentation.

Here's how to upload a mobile photo:

1. **Make sure you have a phone with a camera and you know how to use it to take a picture and/or take a video.**

2. **Go to the Mobile tab of your Account Settings page.**

   You can use this address to get there: `www.face book.com/settings?tab=mobile`.

   There are a few different sections on this page (assuming you've already activated Facebook Mobile). Look for the Post By Email Address section. There should be an e-mail listed in this form. `aaa111parsec@m.facebook.com`. You want to add that personal e-mail address to your phone's contacts so you can easily message it in the future.

3. **Wait for something hilarious or beautiful or awesome to happen and then take a picture or video of it.**

4. **Send an e-mail to the address you just found with the picture or video attached.**

   The subject line is the caption, so choose wisely.

5. **(Optional) To make any edits or changes to your mobile photos, go to your photo albums and click the Mobile Uploads album. To make changes to your video, go to the Video application and edit there.**

   Note that the default visibility of your mobile uploads is Everyone.

Mobile Texts

After your phone has been confirmed, Mobile Texts are the most basic way to use Facebook on your phone. You don't need a camera on your phone or a smartphone to get use from Mobile Texts. Using just a simple SMS (Short Message Service) or text message, you can update your status to let people know where you are and what you're up to.

Here are the various actions you can take on Facebook via SMS:

- ✔ **Update your status** by typing your status into the text message. You can type in any sort of phrase and it will appear on your Facebook Profile and in your friends' News Feeds with a little mobile icon next to it so people know you're on the go.

- ✔ **Add a new Facebook friend** by sending **Add** and the person's name. Using your phone to immediately friend a person you meet is less formal than exchanging business cards, less awkward (and more reliable) than exchanging phone numbers, and gives you more flexibility later for how you want to get in touch. However, remember that friending someone from your phone has all the same implications as friending someone from your computer, so add wisely.

- ✔ **Subscribe to a friend's status updates** by sending **subscribe**, followed by your friend's name. If you have a few friends whom you like to hear absolutely everything from, this is a great way to keep up on the go. If you subscribe to a lot of friends' statuses, make sure you have unlimited texting; otherwise, charges could pile up quickly.

- ✔ **Unsubscribe from a friend's updates** by sending **unsubscribe** followed by their name. Remember the last paragraph, where we said that charges for subscribing to a friend's status could pile up quickly? If you realize you want fewer people's statuses coming straight to your phone, just unsubscribe from the ones you don't want to see on your phone.

✔ **Stop getting texts** by texting the word **stop**.

✔ **Restart getting texts** by texting the word **on**.

What's all the buzz about?

To activate Facebook Mobile Texts, go to the Mobile tab of the Account page; click Edit next to the Notifications section and then select the Text Notifications are On radio button. You can see the Mobile tab in Figure 8-1.

The Notifications section of this page also allows you to control the following options:

✔ **Receive text notifications from friends only**

The text notifications you get can be modified from the Notifications tab of the account Page (more on that in a minute). The Receive Text Notifications from Friends Only check box here controls whether you receive text notifications of message from friends only. This means that if, for example, you get texted whenever you get a new message, you can choose to receive only texts about messages from friends. Messages from strangers won't be texted to you.

✔ **Text times**

You can specify what time you prefer to receive text notifications so, for example, if someone Pokes you at 2 a.m., you don't have to wake up for it. (Maybe you *only* want to know who's trying to Poke you at 2 a.m. No judgment here.)

Additionally, you can opt to not receive text notifications (via the Do not send SMS notifications check box) while you're actively using Facebook because that can get a bit redundant.

✔ Whose Status Updates Should Go to My Phone?

This is another entry point for specifying which of your friends' statuses you want sent to your phone. Simply type the name of the friend you want to subscribe to into this text box and press Enter.

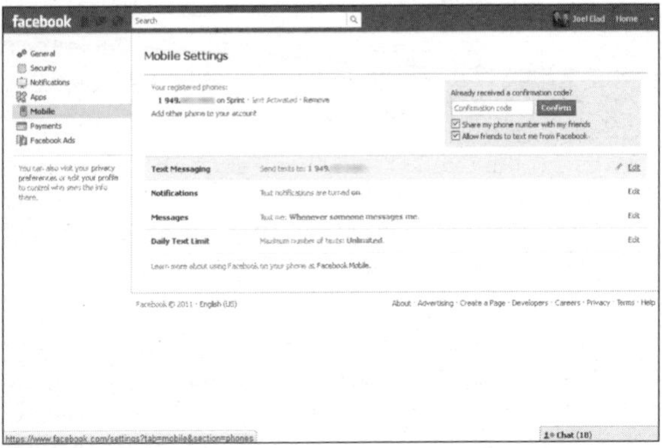

Figure 8-1: Set up your preferences for receiving notifications on your mobile phone.

Using Facebook Mobile

Viewing a web page from your phone can be extremely difficult because the information that is normally spread across the width of a monitor must be packed into one tiny column on your phone. Facebook is no exception to this, which is why the very first tip in this section is this: Never go to www.facebook.com/ on your mobile phone. You'll regret it.

But fear not, you still have a way to carry almost all
the joys of Facebook right in your purse or pocket. On
your mobile phone, open your browser application
and navigate to m.facebook.com — a completely
new window in Facebook designed specifically to
work on a teeny-tiny screen.

If you use an iPhone, Android, or one of a few other
select phone types, navigating to www.facebook.
com/ or m.facebook.com prompts you to install an
app, which I talk about in more detail in the upcoming
"Mobile Apps" section.

The first time you arrive at m.facebook.com, you're
asked to log in. After that, you never (or rarely) have
to reenter your login information unless you explicitly
select Logout from your session, so be sure you trust
anyone to whom you lend your phone.

If you plan to use the Facebook Mobile site frequently, I recommend that you have an unlimited data plan that allows you to spend as much
time on the Mobile Web as you like for a fixed
rate. The Facebook Mobile site is nearly as com-
prehensive and rich as the computer version.
You can spend hours there and, if you're paying
per minute, spend your life savings, too.

Mobile Home

After you log in, you see the mobile version of the
Facebook Home page. Although the design of the
mobile site is somewhat based on the design of the
regular website, it has some significant differences.
Some of the differences exist simply because of less
space; the mobile site must cut to the chase while
allowing you to get more information on a particular
topic.

To follow along with this section, you can navigate to m.facebook.com on your web browser. Just imagine what you see on about one-tenth of the screen.

The Mobile Web page is shown in Figure 8-2. In this section, we detail what you see on the Mobile Home page; we cover the other pages in the following sections.

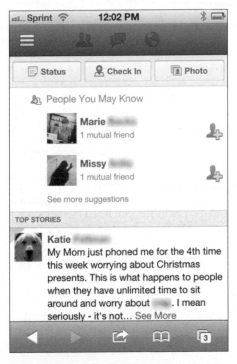

Figure 8-2: Facebook Mobile Home, also known as m.facebook.com.

From m.facebook.com, you'll see these items in your Mobile Home page:

- ✔ **Facebook menu (three horizontal lines):** The three horizontal lines at the top-left corner of the screen represent the drop-down menu with links to the usual Facebook suspects: News Feed, Messages, Places, Events, Friends, Groups, Notes, Settings, and Help.

- ✔ **Friend Requests, Messages, and Notifications:** The three icons across the top of your screen are used throughout the Facebook experience: Friend Requests, Messages, and Notifications. Any unread instances in each category will be marked with the red flag, just like when you log on to your Facebook account from a PC. Tap any of these icons to review that category.

- ✔ **Sort:** This button, at the top right of the screen, allows you to choose whether mobile News Feed shows you Top Stories (stories that Facebook's algorithms believes you will find most interesting) or Most Recent (whatever has just been posted).

- ✔ **New Notifications and Birthdays:** When you reach the mobile site, you find whether you have any upcoming Events or notifications right at the top of the Home page. These links appear only if you have something waiting for you. You will also be notified if any of your friends are celebrating their birthdays today, so you can easily hop over to their Walls and wish them a happy day.

- ✔ **Status box:** When you use Facebook from your mobile phone, you're probably not sitting at your home office, workplace, or school. You may be trapped in jury duty, hanging with friends at a bachelorette party, or waiting in line for a roller coaster. Facebook makes it super-easy to update your status so you can spread the news the moment you're doing something that you want people to know or when you want people to meet you.

✔ **Photo button:** If you want to upload a photo to your Facebook account, you can tap this button and either use your built-in camera to take a photo (or video) or pick a photo from your mobile device photo library to upload to your page.

✔ **Check In button:** If you want to let people know where you are, through Facebook, tap the Check In button to check in with your location and share that status on your Wall.

✔ **Mobile News Feed:** Shows you the most recent stories that you would see on your computer. As you scroll down, you'll get more and more stories, so you can keep reading to your heart's content.

Mobile Timeline

Timelines on Facebook Mobile are designed to more or less work like Timelines on Facebook's regular site, though of course they exist on a tiny screen. When you go to someone's profile, you see his cover and Timeline photos, his basic info, and links to more of his info, just like on the regular site. As you scroll down, you see the same history of posts. You can click to continue browsing through his history.

At the top of his posts are buttons that allow you to post to his Timeline or share a photo with him.

Mobile Inbox

The Mobile Inbox functions the same as the Inbox on the regular site, but you access it in a compacted view. In the Mobile Inbox, your messages are sorted by the time the last message on a thread was sent. Each thread includes the sender's name, the date or how recently the message was sent and a snippet of the message.

When you enter into the mobile thread, similar to regular Facebook, the newest message is at the bottom with the Reply box beneath it. At the top of the message is a link to see older messages in the thread. (Remember, Facebook's message threads include a full history of your communication with a friend. I have friends with message histories that go back *years*.)

In the top-right corner is a button with the mail icon in it (it looks like an envelope with an arrow flying out of it). Click this to access a drop-down menu with action links. You can Mark Read/Unread, Delete, Mark Spam, Move to Other, Archive, Forward or Report Abuse. The Mark as Unread link is particularly handy because often you read a message on your mobile phone, but don't have time or energy to type a response right then. Marking it as Unread reminds you to respond when you return to your computer.

Mobile Apps

Mobile Web and Mobile Texts are generally flexible systems. You can use them from almost any type of phone, with any sort of plan, and they generally look and work the same way. However, mobile apps are a different breed. They are tailor-made by Facebook for specific devices, and the way they work from device to device can differ greatly depending on factors like whether there's a touch screen or not. Right now, Facebook has apps available for the following phone types: iPhone, Palm, Sony Ericsson, INQ, Blackberry, Nokia, Android, Windows Phone, and Sidekick.

The mobile app for each device may look and operate differently. The following section focuses on how the Facebook for iPhone app works; I've checked it against the Android App on the Samsung Galaxy SIII, and they look and feel really similar. So if you have an Android or iPhone, or any phone with a touchscreen, this will be fairly accurate. If you have something more specific, like the Blackberry App, you might have some major differences. Play around with the app to get a feel for the usual functions: Sharing a status, reading the News Feed, Checking out a Profile, and Sending a Message.

iPhone layout

The Facebook app for iPhone is organized exactly like the mobile home page for Facebook. When you tap the top-left corner (represented by the three horizontal bars) of the screen, you see the drop-down menu to access the different parts of Facebook.

✔ **Profile:** This menu option takes you to your own Profile. In general, Profiles are organized into the same Wall, Info, and Photo tabs as Profiles on the site; however, each is abbreviated, and any additional tabs that might exist on the real Profile aren't on this version of the website. The Info tab has only basic and contact information. To add something to your Wall, you can use the Share photo or Write Post button located above your Profile picture.

✔ **News Feed:** News Feed is the same News Feed you see on your computer screen, a constantly updating list of what your friends are up to at this moment. You can comment on and Like posts from News Feed, as well as using the Publisher there to add your own status update or mobile upload.

✔ **Messages:** This is where you access all your messages. From here, you can compose a new message, delete a message, or reply to one. You will also see the number of unread notifications as a number on the right side.

✔ **Nearby:** This is an aspect of Facebook that lets you use your phone's GPS to share or check in where you are with your friends. It's so special that it gets its own section. If you see a number next to Nearby, that shows the number of friends that have checked in close to you recently.

✔ **Events:** This lets you get to any Events you've RSVPed to. This is incredibly useful when it turns out neither you nor your significant other remembered the exact street address of the dinner you're going to.

✔ **Friends:** The Friends section of the iPhone app should feel fairly similar to your phone's contact list. You can scroll through your friends from A to Z or search them from the search box at the top of the list. Any friends who have phone numbers listed have a big phone icon next to their names. Tap the phone icon to initiate a text or phone call.

✔ **Groups:** This lets you interact with any groups you are a part of. This way you don't miss discussions when you're out and about.

✔ **Apps:** This brings you to your own Facebook apps, like Photos, Notes, and anything you installed on your Facebook account that would work on a mobile device.

✔ **Pages and Lists:** These last two options let you go directly to any Pages on Facebook that you follow or any Lists of friends or acquaintances that you have created using Facebook.

At the bottom of the menu is the Account option. This lets you update your Account or Privacy settings, reach the Help center, or log out of your account.

Part IX

Ten Frequently Asked Questions

*H*aving worked for Facebook and worked on this book for several years, I know a lot about the specific complications, confusions, and pain points people come across while using Facebook. At dinner parties, group functions, family events, or even walking across the street wearing a Facebook hoodie, someone always has a suggestion or a question about how to use the site. It's understandable. Facebook is a complex and powerful tool with a ton of social nuances, many of which have yet to be standardized. There are many features, and Facebook changes a lot. Each year, Facebook modifies parts of the site, redesigns how certain pages look and feel, and adds features. To keep up on what's happening with Facebook, you can Like the official Facebook Page, and you'll get updates straight from the horse's mouth.

Is My Computer Infected with a Virus?

One of the main ways that people discover they've picked up a virus through Facebook is when a friend receives a message from them that looks like spam. If this situation happens to you, your first step should be to change your password by clicking the Forgot Your Password link from the login page, or going to Account Settings. Often, viruses hack an account and change the associated e-mail address or password to take control. If you can't change your password, that's probably what happened. If that's the case, contact Facebook customer support immediately by going to the Security Help topic in the Help center: www.facebook.com/help/?page=420. Finally, you should run a virus scan of your computer to help remove any malware that might have ended up on your computer as a result.

Much more information about Facebook-related viruses can be found at www.facebook.com/security.

Do People Know When I Look at Their Timelines?

No. No. No. When people see stories about their friends pop up on their Home page, they sometimes get a little anxious that this means Facebook is tracking everything everyone does and publishing it to everyone else. That's not true. Consider two types of actions on Facebook: creating content and viewing it. Creating content means that you've intentionally added something to Facebook for others to look at or read, such as uploading a photo or a video, commenting or Liking something, or posting a status. These types of actions are all publishable posts — that is, stories about them may end up on your timeline or in your friends' News Feeds — although you have direct control over who sees these posts. The other type of action on Facebook is viewing content such as flipping through photos, watching a video, clicking a link your friend has Liked, or viewing someone's timeline. Unless someone is looking over your shoulder as you browse, these types of actions are strictly private. No one is ever directly notified about them, and no trace of the fact that you took that action is left on your timeline or in your friends' News Feeds. Therefore, you can check people out to your heart's content.

I Have a Problem with My Account — Can You Help Me?

I wish I could. Unfortunately, I'm a user like you, and that means while I can help diagnose the issue, I can't usually treat it. Sometimes the problems are Facebook's fault, and sometimes they are user error, but either way, I don't really have the tools required to fix it. Only employees with special access to the specific tool required to fix an account can resolve account problems. Here are a few of the account questions I've received recently, and the answers given:

- ✔ **I can't remember my password. Can you reset it for me?** Answer: No can do. Click the Forgot Your Password link on the login page to start the reset process, which entails Facebook sending a reset link to your e-mail account.

- ✔ **My account was deactivated because it said I was sending too many messages. Why? Can you fix it?** Answer: I recently had this happen to two friends: one who was using his account to promote his music career, and one who was distributing his poetry to many, many friends through messages. This is Facebook spam detection at work. When an account starts sending a lot of messages in quick succession, especially when those messages contain links, this looks a lot like spam to the system. In most cases, the person is warned, but if the behavior continues, his account is disabled. The only way to have this action reversed is to write in through the Help pages and request reactivation. To write in, click Help Center from the Account menu — the white downward-facing arrow — from the blue bar on top. Search for an FAQ titled My Personal Facebook Account Is Disabled, and follow the instructions for contacting Facebook. This can sometimes take several days.

What Do I Do with Friend Requests I Don't Want to Accept?

This is a tough question. As far as I know, there isn't exactly a social convention for this yet, so the answer to this question is pretty personal. Just know that you can take a number of actions:

✔ **Many people just leave the request sitting there forever.** I don't recommend this action because it just clutters up your account — it's better to make a decision.

✔ **Click Not Now.** This is my favorite option. It sends the request to the hidden requests section of the Friends page, where you won't have to see it anymore. You can then go delete the request from that section of the Friends page. Although people are never directly notified that you've rejected their request, they may notice later that you're not friends and make the correct inference you did not accept. If you do ignore a request, you also need to prepare your follow-up if she asks you about why you ignored her request. Because there is no social convention for this situation just yet, most responses work well here, such as "I'm sorry, I like to keep my friend list down to only my closest friends," or "It's OK. I don't use Facebook often, anyway." You can try "Weird, Facebook must have messed up, I don't think I got it," but then you'll have to accept her request when she likely tries again.

✔ **If you don't want to accept because you don't want that person having access to your timeline, you can accept the request and then add him to a special restricted Friend List, like the acquaintances list.** You can go into your Privacy settings and exclude that Friend List from seeing any parts of your timeline. Then anyone you add to that list will be restricted. In this way, you can accept the friend request without giving up access to your timeline.

✔ **If you don't want to accept because you don't want to read about that person in your News Feed, no problem!** Simply hit Accept. The first time she shows up in News Feed, hit the caron (downward-pointing triangle) at the upper-right of the story and choose Unsubscribe from <friend's name> or Hide All by <friend's name>. This action removes her from your News Feed for good until you choose to add her back.

What's the Difference between Facebook, MySpace, Twitter, and LinkedIn?

It's likely there are graduate students across the globe writing theses on this particular topic. It's a tough question to answer in a paragraph or casual conversation, so anything you read here is a gross generalization and subject to opinion:

- **MySpace has its origins as a tool for local bands to promote their music.** Because many people love music, many people flocked to MySpace (www.myspace.com) in order to connect with their favorite musical artists. A key rule of advertising is to go where the people are, and because so many people were going to MySpace, other businesses and celebrities got involved to garner public attention as well. To this day, MySpace is still oriented toward the relationships between people and media and people and celebrities. The site is designed in a way to make it maximally easy for popular figures to achieve wide distribution and large audiences, or even for everyday Janes and Joes to become popular figures.

- **LinkedIn is a tool geared to help people connect primarily for business purposes.** LinkedIn (www.linkedin.com) users try to connect with as many people as they can so that when they need a new job or they're looking for someone to hire, they can flip through a vast network of friends and friends of friends to find a reliable lead. People can write and request letters of recommendation for one another, and often recruiters reach out to LinkedIn users whether they're actively looking for a job or not.

✔ **Twitter allows people to engage in real-time sharing.** Whenever a Twitter member has something interesting to share, he blasts out some text, 140 characters or fewer, that everyone who is "following" him has the option to see. The Twitter post is actually very similar to a Facebook Status Update. What differentiates Twitter (www.twitter.com) from Facebook is its extreme simplicity and single focus on real-time exchange of ideas. Facebook is a place where you build longstanding relationships with people; you have access to their static content like their phone numbers and photos; you can message them privately or interact with them through groups and events. Twitter is a place where your friends (and anyone else) find out the information you're sharing at any given time, and vice versa. Popular uses of Twitter are link sharing for interesting websites and news, short opinions about current events, and enabling people to meet up when two people are out and about at the same time.

Will Facebook Start Charging Me to Use the Site?

Another simple answer: No.

This rumor is a particularly nasty one that makes the rounds every now and again via people's statuses. There are several variations, but they always seem to involve asking you to repost the status that Facebook is shutting down/going to start charging/running out of names. Don't fall victim to this ruse. Facebook has long maintained that it will always be free to users. Unless you're advertising something, Facebook will always have free space for you.

How Do I Convince My Friends to Join Facebook?

Most methods for persuasion involve showing (rather than telling) your friend the value by sending him links to the photos you post on Facebook, putting his e-mail address on the invite of Event and group invitations, or even sending him links and messages (again, by putting his e-mail address on the To line) from the Facebook Inbox.

You can tell her anecdotally the ways in which Facebook has enriched your life. Maybe you're interacting with your kids more, you're keeping in touch with friends you thought were lost, or you have a place to put your thoughts and photos where your friends might actually see them. You can let her look over your shoulder as you use the site so that she can see the experience herself — ask her questions about whether there's anyone in particular she'd like to look up. The more information she sees about the people she cares about, the more likely she is to take the next step.

One common complaint from people who haven't joined the site is that they "don't have time for yet another computer thing." To this concern, one common response is that Facebook is an efficiency tool that often saves a person time compared to using old-school methods. Messaging can often replace e-mail, and events are easier to coordinate over Facebook. Sharing phone numbers is easier. Sending and receiving links is easier. Finding rides to the airport, restaurant recommendations, and who is heading to the park on Saturday are all faster and easier than trying to use e-mail, phone, or other methods of communication.

What if 1 Don't Want Everyone Knowing My Business?

You can be an extremely private person and still derive nearly all the same value out of Facebook as anyone else. All you have to do is learn how to use the Privacy controls and lock down all your information and access to your timeline, ensuring that only those you trust can see your info. From there, you can interact in all the same ways as anyone else without feeling like your privacy is being compromised.

1 Heard Facebook Owns Everything 1 Put on Its Site — True?

In a legal sense, yes. You also own everything you put on Facebook, and whenever you delete any of your content, Facebook will delete it. What Facebook doesn't own (but you do) is the right to transfer ownership of any of your content to anyone else. Therefore, it's illegal for anyone else to take your content from Facebook and use it for his or her own or any commercial use. In early 2009, many Facebook users banded together to express concern about who owned their content. In response, Facebook published a Statement of Rights and Responsibilities that makes a commitment about what Facebook will and won't do with your information. Every Facebook user who chose to participate voted on these commitments, which govern the company's use of any material you add to the site. Read about these rights and responsibilities in detail at www.facebook.com/terms.

Does Facebook Have a Feature That Lets Me Lock Myself Out for a Few Hours?

Short answer: not really.

Long answer: Many people do *deactivate* their accounts. Deactivation is a way of shutting down your account temporarily. It means that no one will see your timeline or be able to interact with you on Facebook. Some people will deactivate their accounts, their reason being "I spend too much time using Facebook." The benefit of such an action is that you're guaranteed not to get notifications about messages, picture tags, timeline posts, or anything else. The downside is that it will cause a lot of confusion among your friends who suddenly can't message you, tag you, or write on your timeline. If they have your e-mail address, they're likely to bug you anyway to ask why you disappeared from Facebook.

The reason it's not a real solution is that all you have to do to reactivate at any time is to enter your password (just like signing in), and you're completely back to normal. Therefore, if you're remotely curious how your social group has evolved without you, you might have trouble truly staying away. Which brings me to my next suggestion: Have some self-control. Just like many good things in life, the key to keeping them good is moderation. French fries are delicious, but too many give you a tummy ache. Dancing is a blast 'til your feet are covered with blisters. Television is educational and entertaining until it's

3 a.m., you're watching your fifth infomercial, you forgot to feed the cat and put out the trash, and you find yourself wondering what life is all about. Facebook is no different. It's a brilliant utility when used to make your life easier and your social interactions richer. When you find yourself flipping through two-year-old vacation photos of a friend of a friend of a friend of a friend, it's time to blink a few times, step away from the mouse, and go out for ice cream, or dancing, or whatever else it is that gives you joy.

Apple & Macs

iPad For Dummies,
2nd Edition
978-1-118-02444-7

iPhone For Dummies,
5th Edition
978-1-118-03671-6

iPod touch For Dummies,
3rd Edition
978-1-118-12960-9

Mac OS X Lion
For Dummies
978-1-118-02205-4

Blogging & Social Media

CityVille For Dummies
978-1-118-08337-6

Facebook For Dummies,
4th Edition
978-1-118-09562-1

Mom Blogging
For Dummies
978-1-118-03843-7

Twitter For Dummies,
2nd Edition
978-0-470-76879-2

WordPress
For Dummies,
4th Edition
978-1-118-07342-1

Business

Cash Flow For Dummies
978-1-118-01850-7

Investing For Dummies,
6th Edition
978-0-470-90545-6

Job Searching
with Social Media
For Dummies
978-1-118-93072-4

QuickBooks 2011
For Dummies
978-0-470-64649-6

Resumes For Dummies,
6th Edition
978-0-470-87361-8

Starting an Etsy Business
For Dummies
978-0-470-93067-0

Cooking & Entertaining

Cooking Basics
For Dummies, 4th Edition
978-0-470-91388-8

Wine For Dummies,
4th Edition
978-0-470-04579-4

Diet & Nutrition

Kettlebells For Dummies
978-0-470-59929-7

Nutrition For Dummies,
5th Edition
978-0-470-93231-5

Restaurant Calorie
Counter For Dummies,
2nd Edition
978-0-470-64405-8

Digital Photography

Digital SLR Cameras &
Photography
For Dummies, 4th Edition
978-1-118-14489-3

Digital SLR Settings
& Shortcuts
For Dummies
978-0-470-91763-3

Photoshop Elements 9
For Dummies
978-0-470-87872-9

Gardening

Gardening Basics
For Dummies
978-0-470-03749-2

Vegetable Gardening
For Dummies,
2nd Edition
978-0-470-49870-5

Green/Sustainable

Raising Chickens
For Dummies
978-0-470-46544-8

Green Cleaning
For Dummies
978-0-470-39106-8

Health

Diabetes
For Dummies,
3rd Edition
978-0-470-27086-8

Food Allergies
For Dummies
978-0-470-09584-3

Living Gluten-Free
For Dummies,
2nd Edition
978-0-470-58589-4

Hobbies

Beekeeping
For Dummies,
2nd Edition
978-0-470-43065-1

Chess For Dummies,
3rd Edition
978-1-118-01695-4

Drawing For Dummies,
2nd Edition
978-0-470-61842-4

eBay For Dummies,
7th Edition
978-1-118-09806-6

Knitting
For Dummies,
2nd Edition
978-0-470-28747-7

Language &
Foreign Language

English Grammar
For Dummies,
2nd Edition
978-0-470-54664-2

French For Dummies,
2nd Edition
978-1-118-00464-7

German For Dummies,
2nd Edition
978-0-470-90101-4

Spanish Essentials
For Dummies
978-0-470-63751-7

Spanish For Dummies,
2nd Edition
978-0-470-87855-2

Available wherever books are sold. For more information or to order direct: U.S. customers visit
www.dummies.com or call 1-877-762-2974. U.K. customers visit www.wileyeurope.com or
call (0) 1243 843291. Canadian customers visit www.wiley.ca or call 1-800-567-4797.
Connect with us online at www.facebook.com/fordummies or @fordummies

Math & Science

Algebra I For Dummies,
2nd Edition
978-0-470-55964-2

Biology For Dummies,
2nd Edition
978-0-470-59875-7

Chemistry For Dummies,
2nd Edition
978-1-1180-0730-3

Geometry For Dummies,
2nd Edition
978-0-470-08946-0

Pre-Algebra Essentials
For Dummies
978-0-470-61838-7

Microsoft Office

Excel 2010 For Dummies
978-0-470-48953-6

Office 2010 All-in-One
For Dummies
978-0-470-49748-7

Office 2011 for Mac
For Dummies
978-0-470-87869-9

Word 2010
For Dummies
978-0-470-48772-3

Music

Guitar For Dummies,
2nd Edition
978-0-7645-9904-0

Clarinet For Dummies
978-0-470-58477-4

iPod & iTunes
For Dummies, 9th Edition
978-1-118-13060-5

Pets

Cats For Dummies,
2nd Edition
978-0-7645-5275-5

Dogs All-in-One
For Dummies
978-0470-52978-2

Saltwater Aquariums
For Dummies,
2nd Edition
978-0-470-06805-2

Religion & Inspiration

The Bible For Dummies
978-0-7645-5296-0

Catholicism
For Dummies,
2nd Edition
978-1-118-07778-8

Spirituality For Dummies,
2nd Edition
978-0-470-19142-2

Self-Help &
Relationships

Happiness For Dummies
978-0-470-28171-0

Overcoming Anxiety
For Dummies,
2nd Edition
978-0-470-57441-6

Seniors

Crosswords For Seniors
For Dummies
978-0-470-49157-7

iPad For Seniors
For Dummies, 2nd Edition
978-1-118-03827-7

Laptops & Tablets
For Seniors
For Dummies,
2nd Edition
978-1-118-09596-6

Smartphones & Tablets

BlackBerry
For Dummies, 5th Edition
978-1-118-10035-6

Droid X2 For Dummies
978-1-118-14864-8

HTC ThunderBolt
For Dummies
978-1-118-07601-9

MOTOROLA XOOM
For Dummies
978-1-118-08835-7

Sports

Basketball For Dummies,
3rd Edition
978-1-118-07374-2

Football For Dummies,
4th Edition
978-1-118-01261-1

Golf For Dummies,
4th Edition
978-0-470-88279-5

Test Prep

ACT For Dummies,
5th Edition
978-1-118-01259-8

ASVAB For Dummies,
3rd Edition
978-0-470-63760-9

The GRE Test
For Dummies, 7th Edition
978-0-470-00919-2

Police Officer Exam
For Dummies
978-0-470-88724-0

Series 7 Exam
For Dummies
978-0-470-09932-2

Web Development

HTML, CSS, & XHTML
For Dummies, 7th Edition
978-0-470-91659-9

Drupal For Dummies,
2nd Edition
978-1-118-08348-2

Windows 7

Windows 7
For Dummies
978-0-470-49743-2

Windows 7
For Dummies,
Book + DVD Bundle
978-0-470-52398-8

Windows 7 All-in-One
For Dummies
978-0-470-48763-1

Available wherever books are sold. For more information or to order direct: U.S. customers visit
www.dummies.com or call 1-877-762-2974. U.K. customers visit www.wileyeurope.com or
call (0) 1243 843291. Canadian customers visit www.wiley.ca or call 1-800-567-4797.
Connect with us online at www.facebook.com/fordummies or @fordummies

Wherever you are
in life, Dummies
makes it easier.

From fashion to Facebook®,
wine to Windows®,
and everything in between,
Dummies makes it easier.

Visit us at Dummies.com and connect with us online at
www.facebook.com/fordummies or @fordummies

Dummies products make life easier!

- DIY
- Consumer Electronics
- Crafts
- Software
- Cookware

- Hobbies
- Videos
- Music
- Games
- and More!

For more information, go to **Dummies.com**® and search the store by category.

Connect with us online at www.facebook.com/fordummies or @fordummies